Second Helpings

The Southern Eatin' Cookbook

Published by
Darrell and Lisa Huckaby

2755 Ebenezer Rd.
Conyers, GA 30094

1st Edition
1st Printing

Huckaby, Darrell and Lisa
Second Helpings
Copyright 2011
All rights reserved
Printed in the United States of America

Cover Design by The Adsmith, Inc.
Athens, GA

ISBN 978-0-615-46107-6

Second Helpings

The Southern Eatin' Cookbook

by

Darrell Huckaby

and his lovely wife Lisa

Our Heavenly Father,

accept our thanks for these and all our many blessings.

We humbly beg for Christ's sake.

Amen

For Ben Evans

The best produce man in the world.

Darrell and Lisa Huckaby

This is about the tenth book we have done together. The fact that you are holding it in your hand and reading right now is a testament to the miraculous power of love—because if we didn't love one another, one of us would not have survived doing this book together. Trust me, we are not two peas in a pod. But I, Darrell, could not have survived all these years without my lovely wife whom God sent to complete me.

I must make a couple of disclaimers before we get started. I have tried to make cooking an exact science, but we all know that it is not. When we say to cook something for 40 minutes at 350 degrees and you do that, if it doesn't look done, please cook it a while longer. By the same token, if we have suggested you fry a catfish filet for seven minutes and it looks done after five, please don't burn it to a crisp. Or if you do, please don't blame us.

I wanted to write this book because I like to eat and I like to talk about eating and I have discovered, over the years, that most Southerners do, too. If you enjoy having this cookbook, please tell your friends about it. And if you get really good at cooking something in it, don't be shy about inviting us over to try it. We just might come.

Table of Contents

Put a Little South in your mouth!

This ain't exactly a cookbook, y'all. It is more a book about cooking. Or maybe I should say it is a book about eatin'—the way Southerners do it—or used to do it. There is sure to be a great deal of nostalgia once I start thinking about food, which is one of my three favorite subjects. The others are Georgia football and--well, never mind.

This isn't my first stab at writing a cookbook. In 1999 I published *Dinner on the Grounds*, a collection of recipes and funny stories from old fashioned church dinners. I'm talking about the kind where the ladies of the church would get up at the crack of dawn and make their very best recipes. Tables would be laden with deviled eggs and potato salad and green bean casseroles and everything else you could think of to put in your mouth. Once the preacher said grace, the ladies would stand back and watch, paying close attention to whose fried chicken or creamed corn disappeared first, even though they would never admit it.

Well, this collection of recipes and stories goes beyond the church grounds and fellowship halls of the local church and into the homes and backyards of salt-of-the-earth, everyday people—good Southern people who are proud of their heritage. These recipes come from folks who remember when frying in lard and seasoning with salt pork was a way of life.

Some of the dishes are as plain as white bread. Others are fancy enough for out-of-town company. We have recipes for weeknight suppers and Easter brunch and every occasion in between—tailgate parties, outdoor cookouts, fish fries and late-night snacks. If you can think of a reason to have a bite to eat, we will probably cover it in the pages of this book. And if we don't—well, send us your own recipes because there is probably a third Huckaby cookbook lurking out there somewhere.

Let me tell you how this book came about. It had been in the planning stage for a while—and by planning stage, I mean that I had been thinking about it in the back of my mind. I had even collected a recipe or two. And then one day at school—not to be confused with "this one time at band camp"—my lunch group was talking about that one dish that just made Thanksgiving. You know the dish I am talking about. I am talking about Aunt Gladys's sweet potato pie or Granny's dressing or sister Sue's green beans—those dishes.

The conversation motivated me to go ahead and pursue the cookbook I had been planning all along--so naturally the folks at my table are taking credit for this publication. And since they are, I suppose it is only fitting that I tell you a little about the group.

When you teach hormone-laden teenagers for a living, lunch is an important part of the day. That twenty minutes of adult conversation can sometimes be the difference between survival and whatever the alternative might be. So we have rules at our table. No negative comments allowed. And we can't talk about school. Period.

We are a pretty eclectic group. There is Greg, who is the principal and technically our boss—but he's not the real bossy type unless he has to be and if he feels the need to be bossy during lunch, he just stays away.

Then there is Jim. He and I are on different ends of the political spectrum but we enjoy one another's company—so we don't talk politics during lunch. We can talk about food—and do.

Peggy is an Alabama girl who is on loan to us from Dothan. She is one of the best listeners I have ever known and remembers everything anyone ever says about their families or pets or—well, anything. Like Greg, she is an Alabama fan, so football is an important part of our conversation.

Nancy is a Mississippi State fan and can hold her own during the football conversation. She was a lot more fun to have at the table before her son enrolled at Auburn. Julie doesn't like to talk about football at all—or any other sport. Sometimes we let her have her way—between bowl season and spring football.

Terri is the quiet one and listens to whatever we want to talk about. Jennifer is the token Yankee in our group. Every table has to have one, you know. She and I are about as opposite as two people can be—but we've learned to tolerate our differences and enjoy one another's company.

So that's the "quilting circle" as Greg calls us. So, if you like this book—thank them for giving me the inspiration. And if you don't like this book? Just keep it to yourself. No negativity allowed—remember? At any rate, never let it be said that I don't give credit where credit is due. Now please-- kick back and enjoy and as they say across the pond—Bon Appetite, y'all.

Breakfast

is Ready !

Breakfast is Ready!

They don't call it the most important meal of the day for nothing! Of course, way too many of us are in way too big a hurry to do justice to breakfast anymore. It didn't used to be that way you know. Back when I was growing up we had a big breakfast almost every day. You wouldn't find any Kellogg's Corn Flakes in our pantry—much less Fruit Loops and Cap'n Crunch and whatever sugary poisons kids eat these days.

We had bacon and eggs and grits and toast—or maybe pancakes and sausage—always Holifield Farms, by the way—or on really special occasions, country ham and homemade biscuits—and red-eye gravy, of course. We usually had fruit, too. You could count on fresh cut cantaloupe in the summer—or maybe fresh strawberries or blackberries—and Florida grapefruit in the winter. Are you hungry yet?

I hope so.

Now honesty compels me to admit that my own children were not as lucky growing up as I was. They had more than their share of processed cereal and Pop Tarts and such, and the most creative thing I did for them at breakfast time was put their initials on the Toaster Strudel with white icing. And I don't expect folks to get up at the crack of dawn and cook a big country breakfast every day. But, hopefully, this section of the book will put you in a mind to heat up the skillet, at least every once in a while.

Dig in!

Basic Bacon and Eggs

Let's face it. Nothing says breakfast like bacon and eggs and you might be thinking, "Anybody can cook bacon and eggs." But you might be surprised how many folks can't—or, worse yet—have never tried. And you'd be even more surprise how many folks only cook scrambled eggs because they don't know how to cook them any other way. So why not start at the beginning? It's a very good place to start. When we count we begin with A, B, C; when we sing we begin with Do, Re, Mi. And when we cook breakfast, we begin with B and E. (That's bacon and eggs, in case you are slow to catch on.)

Darrell's Fried Bacon

First of all, start with good bacon. Pay the extra dollar. Buy Oscar Mayer or Hormel Black Label or one of the premium brands. Smith-field will do in a pinch and, depending on where you live, you might have your own favorite brand. The better the bacon, the less likely it is to spatter or shrivel up.

8 to 12 strips of bacon

Start with a cold frying pan. Put bacon on a hot pan and it will bunch up like Hattie Mae Humphrey's underdrawers. Allow at least three strips per person—two because that's a decent serving and at least one more because it smells so good cooking. Stretch the bacon out flat on the pan—or griddle—and turn the heat under the pan to medium. Be patient. Take your time and turn the bacon often. The higher the heat the more crisp the bacon will be—and the more likely you are to wind up with burned bacon. If the bacon stops sizzling, that means that the water has cooked out of it and it is cooking faster. Be extra particular that you don't let it burn.

When the bacon is cooked throughout, drain on paper towels and serve. If you are cooking for a crowd, drain the grease from the first batch and clean the pan with paper towels before starting the second batch. Even if you aren't cooking for a crowd you might want to cook a second batch, just because it tastes so good.

Makes 4-5 servings

o *Company Scrambled Eggs*

8 large eggs

¼ cup milk

1 tbsp butter

4 dashes of salt

Place large frying pan over medium heat. Break eggs into large mixing bowl. Whisk the eggs briskly while adding the milk and salt. Continue to whisk the egg mixture for two minutes, until the color is uniform and the texture is frothy.

Add butter to frying pan and allow to melt, turning pan to allow butter to cover the whole pan. Add the egg mixture, but do not stir immediately. As the eggs begin to set just a bit, drag a spatula or wooden spoon across the eggs, pushing the runny part of the eggs toward the middle. Don't overdo this as it will make the eggs tough. Use the spoon or spatula to break apart large clumps. When eggs are cooked to desired doneness, spoon 'em up into a serving plate or bowl and season with salt and black pepper.

Makes 4-5 servings

Homestyle Scrambled Eggs

8 large eggs, depending on who is eating

1-2 tbsp bacon drippings

salt and pepper

After cooking your bacon, keep a tablespoon or two of the bacon grease in the hot pan

Crack eggs, one at a time, into the frying pan. Drag a spatula or spoon across the eggs, pushing the runny part toward the middle and breaking up the large clumps. Remove from pan when done and sprinkle with salt and pepper. These eggs won't be as fluffy and pretty as the fancy ones you fix for company, but the bacon drippings add flavor and make them sho' nuff good.

Feeds 4-5

Bacon Scramble with Eggs

This is a quick and easy way to cook bacon and eggs for a crowd—like when your kid has a sleepover and it's up to you to fix breakfast.

1 lb bacon

1 dozen large eggs

salt and pepper

Crack the eggs into a large bowl and stir with a whisk for a couple of minutes. Take a pound of bacon and cut each strip into three short pieces. Toss the bacon into a large cold frying pan and turn heat up to medium. You do not have to lay the bacon out in strips for this dish. Rather, sautee or stir-fry the bacon. When the bacon is almost brown, pour off the excess bacon fat and then pour the eggs into the pan and scramble along with the bacon. When eggs are done, take up into a bowl, sprinkle with salt and pepper and serve.

Feeds 6-7

Fried Eggs Over Easy (or medium or well)

A lot of folks I know order their eggs over easy or over medium when they eat out—or maybe even sunny side up—but just scramble them at home because they just aren't confident enough to try anything else at the house. But all it takes is a little practice. You probably want to start with one at a time. Pretty soon you will be doing doubles.

1 egg

1 tbsp butter

Get your pan medium hot, so that the egg will seem to cackle like a hen when you break it into the pan. Just hearing that sound makes me salivate. Melt the butter in the pan by turning the pan from side to side, allowing the melting butter to spread all over the bottom of the pan.

Crack your egg (or eggs, if you have graduated to that point) on the side of the pan and then let it slide out onto the hot pan, being careful not to break the yoke. When the white part of the egg is firm and the yolk is still a lot like jelly, slide a spatula under the egg and carefully roll it over. Don't pick it up and flip it. If you do the yolk is sure to break. Let the egg cook one more minute and then carefully pick it up with the spatula and slide it onto a plate. Sprinkle with salt and pepper.

If the egg is cooked over easy the yellow part will be fairly runny when you cut into it with a fork. I don't like mine to run. I'd prefer that it crawl, which is what most folks would call having it over-medium. If you like your yolk to be firm, just cook it a little longer before flipping it.

If the yolk breaks when you flip it, go ahead and scramble the thing. It will still taste good and you'll get it right next time!

2 of these feeds one.

Scrambled Eggs 'n' Cheese

8 eggs

¼ cup milk

1 cup sharp cheddar cheese

2 tbsp butter

salt and pepper

Crack the eggs into a large bowl and whisk for two minutes, adding milk and salt as you go. Melt butter in skillet over medium heat. Pour egg mixture into pan. Allow eggs to firm up and then slowly drag spatula or wooden spoon over the eggs, pushing runny part toward the middle and breaking up clumps. When eggs are beginning to solidify, sprinkle cheese over eggs and continue to scramble until cheese is melted. Don't leave over heat too long as eggs continue to cook after being removed from heat. Remove from pan into bowl and sprinkle with salt and pepper. Serve hot with bacon or sausage, grits and biscuits and muscadine jelly. Better than snuff and not half as dusty!

Feeds 4-5

Porterdale Omelet

Another way to enjoy eggs is by making them into omelets. A lot of people shy away from omelets because they don't think they know how to make them, but making omelets is just like anything else. Nobody is good at it the first time they try, but all it takes is a little bit of practice and you'll be an old pro in no time. Give it a try. This will get you started.

> **1 tbsp butter**
>
> **3 large eggs**
>
> **¼ cup finely chopped green peppers**
>
> **¼ cup finely chopped onions**
>
> **¼ cup sliced mushrooms**
>
> **¼ cup milk**
>
> **½ cup finely chopped ham**
>
> **¼ cup shredded cheddar cheese**
>
> **salt and pepper**

Break the eggs into a large bowl, add the milk and beat with a whisk until well blended. Two minutes or so should do the trick. Melt the butter in a non-stick skillet. You want to keep your black cast iron skillet in the cabinet when you are making omelets. Pour the peppers, onions and mushrooms into the melted butter and cook over medium heat until tender. This should take about two minutes, too. Pour the egg mixture into the pan. Use a spatula to gently stir the eggs, pushing the runny part toward the center. When the eggs start to firm up, sprinkle the cheese over what is becoming your omelet and add the ham. Add salt and pepper. When the eggs turn white and the edges get a little crispy, slide your spatula under the eggs and either fold one side over the other, or—if you are brave enough—slide the spatula all the way under and flip the omelet over. Cook about 30 more seconds and remove to a serving plate. Of course you are free to experiment with any combination of vegetables and meats and use more or less of each to suit your own taste buds.

Makes 1 3-egg omelet

Daddy Darrell's Pizza Omelet

What can I say? My kids loved pizza. I wanted them to experience the joy of omelets for breakfast. Enough said. It worked.

¾ tbsp butter

2 large eggs

¼ cup finely chopped onions

¼ cup sliced mushrooms

¼ cup milk

½ cup cooked pepperoni slices, cut into halves

¼ cup shredded Mozzarella cheese

salt and pepper

Break the eggs into a large bowl, add the milk and beat with a whisk until well blended. Two minutes or so should do the trick. Melt the butter in a non-stick skillet. You want to keep your black cast iron skillet in the cabinet when you are making omelets. Pour the onions and mushrooms into the melted butter and cook over medium heat until tender. This should take about two minutes, too. Pour the egg mixture into the pan. Use a spatula to gently stir the eggs, pushing the runny part toward the center. When the eggs start to firm up, sprinkle the cheese over what is becoming your omelet and add the pepperoni. Add salt and pepper. When the eggs turn white and the edges get a little crispy, slide your spatula under the eggs and either fold one side over the other, or—if you are brave enough—slide the spatula all the way under and flip the omelet over. Cook about 30 more seconds and remove to a serving plate. Of course you are free to experiment with any combination of vegetables and meats—yes, Italian sausage and/ or ground beef is great. You can even use chopped olives if you dare. If it's good on a pizza it is probably good in an omelet. I would stay away from the anchovies though, if you want the kids to eat them.

Makes 1 2-egg omelet (Duh!)

Homer Huckaby's Hot Cakes and Sausage

My daddy loved to cook breakfast and on Sundays he loved to make pancakes (he ALWAYS referred to them as hot cakes) and he always insisted that sausage, not bacon, was the perfect accompaniment to his hot cakes. We always used Holifield Farm pure pork sausage, and my family still does. We prefer the *hot*, although if my son Jackson had his way we'd buy the *mo pepper* version. But it's all good. I mean it really is.

Fried Sausage Patties

1 lb Holifield Farm sausage (or your favorite brand of bulk sausage)

Pinch off small pieces of sausage (about 2 ½ to 3 ounces). Roll each portion between your palms and then flatten out into patties. You may cook a half pound at a time if you don't have a big crowd on hand. Place patties in a cold frying pan and cook over low heat, turning frequently. The sausage will be very brown on the outside by the time it is done on the inside. If you cook it too fast it will burn on the outside before it is done in the middle.

When sausage is done, drain on paper towels and keep it warm by covering the sausage with a pie plate until the hot cakes are done.

Half a pound feeds 3-4

Homer's Hot Cakes

1 egg

1 cup buttermilk

½ tsp baking soda

1 cup plain flour

1 tbsp melted butter (may substitute cooking oil)

1 tsp sugar

1 tsp baking powder

½ tsp salt

Beat the egg and then add the buttermilk and baking soda. Stir in the flour and next four ingredients. Beat until the batter is smooth and the lumps are gone. Heat a flat pan or griddle to medium and pour a small amount of oil to cover. Pour enough of the batter onto the pan to make about a three or four inch circle when it spreads out. When edges start to turn and bubbles form in the middle, slide a spatula under the pancakes and flip them once. Cook on the other side and remove to a warm plate. On a normal size griddle pan you can cook about three hotcakes at a time. Serve with butter and syrup and sausage. (Honesty compels me to admit that nowadays when we make pancakes, we use Bisquick and plain milk, but these are stomp down good if you take the time to master them.)

Feeds about 4

Easy Waffles

Once in a great while we will have waffles for breakfast instead of pancakes. Truth be known, we have waffles a lot more often on Sunday night, when we like to have "breakfast for supper." Whenever you decide to make them, they are stomp down good. Of course you will need to have a waffle iron. Ours has a non-stick service and makes two waffles at a time.

2 cups plain flour

1 tbsp baking powder

OR

2 cups Bisquick

1 ½ cups milk (maybe a touch less)

1 large egg

Spray your waffle iron with Pam and heat it up. Mix all the ingredients together and pour onto the waffle iron. Bake about five minutes and serve with butter and whatever kind of syrup you like best. Lisa likes them with peanut butter! We also like them with fried bacon and slices of extra sharp cheddar cheese.

Extra Special Pecan Waffles

Make these from scratch when you really want to impress the folks eating with you.

2 eggs

1 ½ cups milk

¼ cup vegetable oil

2 cups all purpose flour

1 tbsp baking powder

1 tsp sugar

¼ tsp salt

1 cup crushed pecans

Combine the eggs, milk and oil in a large bowl. Beat until the ingredients are well mixed and right smooth. You don't want lumps, in other words. Then beat in the flour, baking powder, sugar and salt. Preheat your waffle iron and pour on enough batter to cover. Sprinkle a few of the pecans on top of the mixture. Close the waffle iron and bake until done—about five minutes. Serve with your favorite syrup.

Saturday Morning French Toast

Ever since I saw Dustin Hoffman in *Kramer vs Kramer*, first struggling with and later perfecting the art of making French toast, I have enjoyed making it myself. It is especially good when made with thick slices of bread.

2 eggs

½ cup milk

½ tsp vanilla extract

¼ tsp cinnamon

1 tbsp butter

4 thick slices of bread

4 tbsp powdered sugar

Crack the eggs into a mixing bowl and beat well. Mix in the milk, vanilla and cinnamon. Melt the butter in a non-stick skillet. Dunk the bread, one slice at a time, into the egg mixture, making sure that all surfaces of the bread are well-coated. Cook for about 4 minutes on each side and remove from pan. Sprinkle each piece of toast with powdered sugar. Serve with hot syrup.

My Lovely Wife Lisa's Breakfast Casserole

This dish is reserved at our house for special occasions—like Christmas morning and . . .well, we mostly have it on Christmas morning. There are many versions of this casserole and they show up at Sunday School breakfasts and tailgate parties, but you have to be real careful what you put on your plate at those functions. You can get an underdone, runny casserole if you don't watch yourself, or an overdone and tasteless one—which is almost as bad. But if you follow these directions you'll come out smelling like a rose every single time because Lisa's is simply the best. This is another one of those dishes that you will have to start last night if you want to have it this morning.

7 eggs

2 cups half-and-half

8 slices of white bread

2 tbsp butter

½ tsp powdered mustard

1 tsp salt

½ tsp black pepper

1 lb sausage

2 cups shredded cheddar cheese

Brown the sausage, drain well and set aside. Trim the crusts off the bread and place the bread squares in the bottom of a lightly greased 13x9 pan. (Pam works fine, as always.) Lightly butter the bread. Break the eggs into a large bowl and beat thoroughly. Add mustard, salt, pepper and half-and-half. Sprinkle the sausage evenly over the bread. Sprinkle the cheese over the sausage and then pour the egg mixture over the top of the whole thing. Cover the pan with foil and refrigerate overnight.

The next morning, while you are having your first cup of coffee and reading the newspaper, bake in a preheated oven at 350 degrees for 50-60 minutes, until done. Don't take out too soon or the whole concoction might be a bit runny. When done, the casserole will be bubbly on top and a bit brown.

Lisa's Tailgate-Worthy Stone Ground Cheese Grits

Several years ago my family and I were fortunate enough to have been invited to join the Oak Tree Tailgate Gang. I am not sure why we got invited, but I know why we kept getting invited back. Lisa always brings the cheese grits. Master this recipe and you'll never be lonely on game day again. Now this is a recipe for stone ground grits. Nora Mills is our brand of choice. You can use a half-and-half mixture of yellow and white regular grits.

> **1 cup stone ground grits**
>
> **3 cups water**
>
> **1 tsp salt**
>
> **½ tsp black pepper**
>
> **1 cup milk**
>
> **1 stick butter, cut into 1 tbsp slabs**
>
> **6 oz Velveeta cheese, cut into 1 inch cubes**

In a large pot, combine the water, milk, salt and pepper and bring to a rolling boil. Slowly add the grits,stirring constantly, and reduce heat. Allow the grits to simmer for about 30 minutes until thickened. Stir often and don't let the grits stick to the bottom of the pan, which they are wont to do. Add the butter and cheese and continue to cook, stirring well and often, for another 15 minutes or so. If the grits appear to be too thick you might add a bit of milk along, to thin them out.

Serves 6-8 hungry folks and recipe can be easily doubled or tripled if you need to feed a crowd.

Grits is Groceries Quick Grits

I ain't gonna lie and say that at our house we spend an hour making tailgate worthy grits every time we want grits. As my daddy used to say, "Grits is groceries!" They are a staple on any Southern diet and there was a time when people cooked them at home every day. In most real Southern restaurants grits are still served with every breakfast order. The great Baptist preacher, Marshall Edwards, used to tell a story about a fellow who walked into a café in small Southern town and ordered breakfast. When the young waitress brought his food he did not recognize the white accompaniment to his eggs and asked the girl what it was. She said, "Well, those are grits," to which he replied, "I didn't order any grits."

The girl, bewildered, said, "You don't have to order grits. Grits just come."

I think Marshall was attempting to equate Grace with grits, as being something that God is willing to bestow upon us freely.

Now Yankees will make fun of grits. They will ask foolish questions like, "What's a grit?" and then laugh uproariously, as if they were the first person to think of saying that. Then they will insist that they don't like grits because of the texture or because "they don't taste like anything."

These are the same people, keep in mind, that have kept little boys in South Georgia in pocket money for years by buying pine cones and thinking they were porcupine eggs.

At any rate, when you just want a good helping of grits to go with your breakfast, quick grits are just fine—but never, under any circumstances, use instant grits. Here's how I make them.

2 cups water

1 tsp salt

½ cup quick grits (Aunt Jemima can't be beat.)

2 tbsp butter

salt and pepper

In a medium sized boiler, add 1 tsp of salt to the water and bring to a boil. Then slowly stir in the grits. Cover the pot and turn the heat down low. Allow the grits to simmer about ten minutes, stirring often to keep the grits from sticking—which they really like to do. When the grits are almost done, stir in the butter and sprinkle with salt and liberal amounts of black pepper. If you want to melt a bit of cheddar cheese into them or sprinkle some crumbled bacon on top, or even some thinly sliced green onions, it won't hurt. Feel free to experiment and doctor your grits up the way you think you'll like them.

Makes 4 servings

Country Ham and Buttermilk Biscuits

There ain't nothing better than a good ham biscuit with a cup of steaming hot coffee and I am sure just about everyone has his or her favorite places at which to indulge in such a gastronomical treat. Believe it or not, folks used to make ham biscuits at home and seldom did my family, when I was growing up, head to the mountains or Jacksonville Beach without a shoebox full of ham biscuits wrapped in "tin foil" and they would still be nice and warm when we made our first pit stop to sample my mama's wares. You, too, can have the pleasure of a thick slice of country ham and a homemade biscuit. If you decide to eat them separately with, say, eggs and grits, be sure you make the red-eye gravy to go with them.

The Best Biscuits

When my sister-in-law, Terry, came into the family she used to talk about "whomp biscuits," and I had no idea what she was talking about. Then I heard her explain that they were the kind that you peeled out of a can after you had "whomped" the can on the side of the counter to pop those suckers open. Many historians claim that the decline of the South began when the Union forces repulsed Pickett's charge on Cemetery Ridge at Gettysburg. I believe that the real decline of Southern civilization as we know it came when husbands all across the region began waking up to the sound of canned biscuits being whomped against kitchen counters. Nowadays, canned biscuits have given way to frozen store-bought biscuits in many homes and honesty compels me to admit that we have those way more than we have real homemade biscuits—especially at breakfast. But once in a great while—once in a *very* great while--Lisa surprises us with the best homemade biscuits this side of heaven. Here's how she cooks them. Let the salivating begin.

½ cup Crisco shortening

2 cups self rising flour

¾ cup buttermilk

Cut the flour into the shortening. (That means combine the two with a fork or whip until it resembles coarse meal in texture.) Add the buttermilk and mix well. Pour onto a floured cutting board and knead gently several times. Flatten to about ½ inch by pressing gently with fingers. Cut with a 1 ½ to 2 inch round cookie cutter and place on a greased cookie sheet. Bake in preheated oven at 425 degrees until golden brown. This should take 20-25 minutes, but keep your eye on them.

Makes about a dozen biscuits

Southern Fried Country Ham

The trick to having good country ham is buying good country ham. There are places where you can still buy a whole country cured ham, but if you are somebody who would buy a whole country ham you are probably somebody who knows how to cook one. I have never bought one myself, but I buy the center cut slices at the grocery store about every week. If you are a stranger to country ham, please know that it tastes slightly sour, slightly salty and slightly strong—which is what those of us who love it love about it. Some people boil their ham slices and other broil them. I fry mine and this is how.

Six or eight slices of country ham

¼ cup water

1 tsp shortening or cooking oil

You will only need the shortening if the ham is especially lean. Place the ham slices in a frying pan and add the water. A black cast iron skillet is best, but any old frying pan will do. Cook the ham slices over medium-low heat for about ten minutes until browned on each side. Remove to a serving plate. Save what is left in the pan for the fixin's for red-eye gravy.

Feeds about 4 folks

Andrew Jackson Red-eye Gravy

Folks say that red-eye gravy got its name because Old Hickory, Andy Jackson himself, asked for gravy as red as his blood-shot eyes after an all night bender. Now I don't know if there is any truth to that story, but that's what folks say. However it got its name, it goes great with country ham and grits and buttermilk biscuits. There are as many different ways to make it as there are people. Here's how we do it at our house.

The drippings from the ham you just cooked

¼ cup water

¼ cup brewed coffee (or slightly less)

or

¼ cup Coca Cola (yes, I said Coca Cola)

Remove the ham from the skillet. Pour the water and coffee/Coke into the pan. Bring the mixture to a boil and continue scraping the dregs from the bottom of the pan for a couple of minutes. Pour into a bowl and serve. You'll realize why Andrew Jackson was smart enough to become president.

Sawmill Gravy

If you have sausage with your eggs instead of country ham, you might want to make a little sawmill gravy to go with those biscuits. Sawmill gravy is a common term that people apply to a variety of white gravy made with milk and flour.

3 tbsp fat from sausage

3 tbsp flour (give or take; more if gravy needs to be thicker)

1-2 cups milk

salt and pepper

cooked crumbled sausage (optional)

Cook your sausage and remove from pan, leaving about 3 tbsp of fat in the pan with the renderings. Keep the pan over medium heat and sprinkle in about 3 tbsp of all-purpose flour and stir until it begins to brown. Then slowly add the milk, stirring constantly. Sprinkle in the salt and black pepper and stir until the gravy thickens. If you have cooked a little crumbled sausage, add it and stir it in before removing from the heat.

Special Occasion Breakfast Treats

Sometimes you just want to serve something a little different for breakfast. Maybe you have spend-the-night company or maybe one of the kids hosted a sleepover. Or maybe it is your turn to bring the snacks for Sunday school. Whatever the occasion, you are certain to hit a homerun with any of the following breakfast treats.

Bob Bradley's Christmas Morning Omelets

This is one of the neatest things I have ever tried. It is a unique way to do breakfast and a lot of fun. Plus you can do most of the work ahead of time and you can let each person make his or her own omelet. My friends, Bob and Mary Anne Bradley, serve these every Christmas morning. The whole family helps prepare them on Christmas Eve and then they refrigerate them overnight. Then Bob just cooks them all outside on Christmas morning. It's a great tradition. But not to worry—they work well inside on the stove, too.

1 gallon freezer bag per omelet

3 eggs per omelet

shredded cheddar cheese

finely chopped onions

finely chopped peppers

shredded cooked ham

cooked bacon, crumbled

sliced mushrooms

salt and pepper

This really is cool, y'all. Each person will crack 3 eggs into a gallon size freezer bag. (Qt size works with 2 eggs) Then that person will create an omelet by adding cheese or ham or bacon or whatever ingredients float his or her boat. Then they will manipulate the bag to mix all the ingredients, press all the excess air out of the bag and seal it tight. When it is time for breakfast simply bring a large pot of water to a rolling boil. Lower the prepared freezer bags into the boiling water and leave for 13 minutes. Carefully lift each bag out of the boiling water. Open the bags and the omelets will slide right out. Add salt and pepper to taste and you've got breakfast!

Sausage Pinwheels

You will prepare these the night before and bake them when you wake up in the morning. Easy as pie—but it's sausage pinwheels instead.

1 lb bulk sausage

8 oz cream cheese

2 cans Pillsbury Crescent Rolls

Brown the sausage, loose—not in patties--and drain the grease. Spray two sheets of plastic wrap or wax paper with Pam. Spread the rolls out on the plastic wrap and flatten. Spread the cream cheese over the rolls and then sprinkle the cooked sausage evenly over the rolls. Roll each flattened can of dough into a long log and refrigerate overnight.

The next morning, while you are waiting for your coffee to brew, cut the log into ½ inch slices. Spread the slices out on a lightly greased baking sheet (Pam works great) and bake at 350 in preheated oven until brown—about 15 to 20 minutes. You'll be a hero. They go great with coffee or orange juice.

Feeds 8-10 folks, depending

There is an old Southern saying that whoever takes the last biscuit--or sausage pinwheel--has to kiss the cook. That ain't a bad deal, depending, of course, on what the cook might look like!

Margaret Autry's Sausage Cheese Balls

Margaret Holifield was just about the prettiest girl in the Class of '57 at Newton County High School. Her daddy made sausage—the best around. Margaret, who has always been as sweet as she is pretty, married Jeff Autry, who would become my closest friend. Margaret and Jeff and their three sons were like family to me. Margaret taught me many things—including how to make these sausage balls. They are great for a crowd. Enjoy.

1 pound Holifield Farm Sausage (substitute another brand only if you must)

3 cups Bisquick

4 cups shredded cheddar cheese

Mix all ingredients together in a large bowl. You can try to do it with a wooden spoon but you will need a lot of elbow grease. You might be able to use an electric mixer if you have a good one. Whatever you use, be sure to get the ingredients well blended. Once that has been accomplished, pinch off small pieces and roll into ¾ to 1 inch balls.

Place the balls on a lightly greased cookie sheet and bake in preheated oven until golden brown. It will take about 20-25 minutes. Serve warm.

Makes 8-9 dozen

Valentine's Day Delight

I am truly a bacon and eggs and grits kind of guy in the morning time, but occasionally a fellow wakes up with a sweet tooth and oftentimes this occurs when there is not a Krispy Kreme donut shop with the *HOT* sign on anywhere around. And some occasions just call for something sweet. Take Valentine's Day, for instance. My standard Valentine's Day breakfast, for years, has been miniature sausage links, sliced fresh strawberries, and sweet rolls. Yes, sometimes I do settle for the Pillsbury version—sometimes caramel nut and sometimes the orange sweet rolls--but sometimes store-bought just won't do. For those occasions, try out one—or all—of these delectable breakfast delights.

Sweet Dreams Sticky Rolls

Dough

¼ cup warm water

1 package Fleischmann's Yeast (4 ounces)

¼ cup sugar

1 cup milk

4 tbsp butter

3 egg yolks

1 tsp lemon juice

1 tsp salt

4 cups all purpose flour

Filling

½ cup light brown sugar

1 tbsp ground cinnamon

4 tbsp butter

Icing

¾ cup light brown sugar

4 tbsp butter

3 tbsp honey

1 tbsp Caro Syrup (light)

1 cup chopped pecans

This will be one of the most complicated recipes in this book. In fact, you'll do most of the work the night before, but the smiles on the faces of your family as they lick their fingers and ask for seconds will be worth the trouble.

Make the dough by combining the yeast, water and a tsp of sugar in a mixing bowl. Stir until the dry ingredients dissolve and let sit for 5 minutes. Add all of the other ingredients except 1 cup of the flour and mix with an electric mixer on low speed. (Use dough hooks if you have them.) Once all the flour has been added, increase the speed to medium and knead the dough until it is sticky. If the dough is too wet, add a bit more flour as you go. This takes practice, but it really is worth the trouble. Make the dough into a ball and place in a bowl that you have buttered and roll it round and round to coat with the butter. Cover it with plastic wrap and set it aside for an hour or so to let the yeast work. Once the dough has risen, flatten the dough out on a cutting board (sprinkle the board lightly with flour to keep the dough from sticking) and then let it sit for 15 or 20 minutes.

While this is going on, mix the cinnamon and brown sugar. Melt the butter for the filling and keep it separate.

Roll the dough on a cutting board (yes, you will need a real rolling pin) and make about a 12 x 18 inch rectangle. Brush the dough with the melted butter and sprinkle the cinnamon/sugar mixture over the whole thing. Next roll the dough into a long cylinder and place over wax paper with the seam side down. Cut the dough into 15 slices. (I promise it is not as hard as it sounds and once you've done it once or twice it will become second nature to you.)

Now you are going to make your icing in a one quart saucepan. Dump in the butter, honey, syrup and brown sugar and place over low heat, stirring constantly, until the butter and sugar are melted. Be very careful not to let the brown sugar burn.

Don't fret. We are almost done. Pour the icing mixture into a greased 9 x 13 inch pan and sprinkle the chopped pecans on top, spreading them out evenly. Finally, place the dough, flat side down, on top of the icing. Cover with plastic wrap but not too tightly (the buns will continue to rise) and then put them in the refrigerator overnight.

You are guaranteed to have sweet dreams thinking about the wonderful treat you will have the next morning—and most of the work is already done.

Wake up the next morning and turn on the coffee pot. Preheat the oven to 375 and while it is warming up, take the rolls from the refrigerator and remove the plastic wrap. Pour yourself that first cup of coffee and think about how good the sticky rolls are going to smell. They will taste even better!

When the oven is ready, bake rolls for 30 to 35 minutes until golden brown. Remove from the oven and carefully turn upside down on a serving plate. You won't have to call anyone to the table. The aroma from the oven will draw them like flies to honey. You can thank me the next time you see me.

Feeds 6-8

Lisa's Light and Delicious Banana Nut Bread

Butter a slice or three of this delectable delight while it is still warm out of the oven and enjoy it with a hot cup of coffee. It just doesn't get any better.

2 cups flour

2/3 **cup shortening**

1 1/3 **cup sugar (or slightly less to taste)**

2 eggs

3 ripe bananas

1 cup finely chopped pecans

Cream the sugar and shortening. (This means melt the shortening while stirring in the sugar.) Add the eggs and flour. Mash the bananas thoroughly and add bananas to the sugar/shortening mixture. Add the pecans and mix well. Transfer to a loaf pan and bake in a preheated oven at 350 until done—about 45 minutes to an hour. To test for doneness, you can insert a toothpick into the center of the loaf. If it comes out clean you are good to go. Slice and serve warm with butter. Campbell's soup ain't the only thing that's hmmm hmmm good!

Grandmama Bitzi's Sour Cream Coffee Cake

This one is a little bit crumbly and a whole lot good!

½ cup brown sugar

1 ½ tsp cinnamon

1 cup chopped nuts (pecans or walnuts work well)

3 cups plain flour

½ tsp salt

1 tsp baking soda

3 tsp baking powder

1 ½ cup sugar

1 cup butter—softened

1 cup sour cream

1 tsp vanilla extract

3 eggs

Combine brown sugar, cinnamon and nuts in a small bowl and set aside. Sift the flour into a different bowl and add salt, soda, baking powder, and sugar. Add the butter, sour cream and vanilla. Mix on low for 30 seconds, then turn speed to medium and mix for another minute and-and-a-half. Add the eggs, one at a time, and beat for 30 seconds each.

Next spread half the batter into a 13 x 9 lightly greased pan. Sprinkle with half the cinnamon-sugar-nut mixture. Pour the remaining batter on top. Add the rest of the cinnamon-sugar-nut mixture. Bake in a preheated oven at 350 for 50 to 60 minutes.

Serves 8

Blueberry Muffins

1 ¾ cups plain flour

2 ½ tsp baking powder

1/3 cup butter, softened

¾ cup sugar

1 large egg, beaten

¾ cup milk

¼ tsp vanilla

1 cup blueberries (fresh or thawed frozen blueberries)

½ tsp lemon zest

Get your muffin pan ready by spraying lightly with Pam. In a large bowl, sift together the flour, baking powder and salt and set aside. In a different bowl, cream the butter and sugar together and then add the egg, milk and vanilla and stir until everything is well mixed. You can expect a few small lumps. No worries. Add the wet mixture to the dry and fold together by stirring about a dozen strokes. Add the blueberries and lemon zest and stir just enough to get these ingredients evenly distributed. Take a couple of spoons—one for dipping and one for scraping—and fill each muffin compartment about 2/3 full. Bake in a preheated oven at 375 for about 25 minutes.

Makes 12 muffins

In the South you can say just about anything about a person if you just add, "bless her heart!" afterward.

Dolores Evans's Pumpkin Bars

Every year when it is time for folks to buy their Christmas trees I have a book signing at Evans' Market—the best little produce stand in the world. And every time I do, Mr. Ben's wife, Dolores, makes up all kinds of good groceries to spoil me with. These pumpkin bars are one of her many specialties. They are among my favorites, and they will be among yours, too. Dolores says that she bakes and shares pumpkins bars all fall and uses the delicious pumpkins they sell at the market, but she says that canned pumpkin will work, too.

2 cups sugar

4 eggs

2 cups plain flour

½ tsp salt

1 tsp baking soda

2 tsp baking powder

2 tsp ground cinnamon

1 cup oil

2 cups cooked pumpkin

For the icing (Mrs. Evans doubles this recipe.)

1 3 oz. package cream cheese, softened

1 tsp vanilla

¾ stick softened margarine

2 cups powdered sugar

Mix the ingredients and spread on an 18x12 cookie sheet with sides. Bake at 350 for 30 minutes. Cool completely before icing. For icing simply mix the ingredients together. Spread the icing evenly then cut into bars and serve. Enjoy! And if you ever come to one of my book signings at Evans Market and ask nicely, Dolores might share—if I haven't already eaten them all!

"Best" Banana Bread

This is another of Dolores's recipes. I can vouch for it, too.

3 ripe bananas, mashed

½ cup Wesson Oil

2 eggs

2 cups self-rising flour

2 cups sugar

1 cup chopped pecans

Mix the bananas, oil and eggs well. Sift together the flour and sugar. Combine mixture and mix well. Stir in the chopped pecans. Pour everything into a lightly greased pan—a tube pan works well—and bake at 350 for 1 hour.

Let's Do

Lunch!

Let's Do Lunch!

Don't let the title of this chapter fool you. We ain't about to give you a lot of fancy hoity-toity recipes to fix when it is your turn to host the monthly gathering of the Garden Club. Well, actually we are going to give you a lot of recipes that would be fabulous for the Garden Club— or any other group you might want to impress. A few of those gems will be hidden away in this chapter among the potted meat recipes and the forum on slicing bananas into circles or rectangles. But most of those delicacies will appear in a later section—the one about soups, salads and such.

This particular chapter is about real people eating real food for lunch— the meal that occurs in the middle of the day. These recipes are not necessarily about social lunches. They lean more toward the middle of the day meal that satisfies your taste buds and gives you enough energy to do an afternoon's work.

Lunch was the first meal that I learned to make for myself and, quite naturally, most of the time it involved spreading mayonnaise on white bread and adding anything else I could find in the cupboard or refrigerator that might taste good. A lot of the time what I could find was absolutely nothing—except the mayonnaise. Yes, I have eaten many a mayonnaise sandwich—and I am not the only one, either. I know for a fact that Pee Wee Patterson used to eat them and so did B. J. Clements—and B.J. earned a PhD and was my advisor at the University of Georgia, hallowed be thy name.

Once in a great while there might be some leftover chicken in the icebox—which is what we sometimes called our refrigerator, when we weren't referring to it as the Frigidaire, even though ours was a Kenmore or whatever type appliance Sears-Roebuck sold. My mama wasn't real big on buying cold cuts. Every time I read Heidi, or saw it on television—the one with Shirley Temple—I wound up wanting a cheese sandwich, because she and Goat Peter ate cheese and bread for lunch and, yes I have, I have often eaten mustard and ketchup sandwiches and, if your imagination is strong enough, they can taste just like a hamburger. Now I said if your imagination is strong enough.

So in this chapter I will talk about many of the simple meals mill people used to get through the day—and about some of the things my family and I eat for the midday meal. And like I said—there may be a gem or two scattered about as well. It's up to you to find those. Happy hunting and Bon Appetite!

Classic Tomato Sandwich

There is not a Southerner worth his salt that doesn't like a tomato sandwich, and if you run across one that claims he doesn't, either he hasn't been raised right or there is a Yankee in the woodpile somewhere. Now, whatever you do, don't try to make this sandwich before the middle of June. And don't try to make one with a store-bought tomato. A tomato from a produce stand, like Evans Market in Conyers, is fine, as long as you know the proprietor and can trust him to tell you if the tomatoes in question have been vine ripened or not. If not, eat a can of sardines for lunch—or anything except a tomato sandwich.

The best tomato sandwich is the one where you go out and pick the tomato yourself, off your own vine. You can use somebody else's tomatoes if you need to—but only, as I said, if it has been grown in local dirt and allowed to turn red right on the vine. But enough talk. Here we go.

2 slices white bread

mayonnaise

salt and pepper

Variation—Durkee's Special Sauce

Take a freshly picked vine-ripe tomato. Make sure it has been washed. Peel it if you must—this is not really necessary but is purely a matter of choice. My lovely, wife, Lisa always peels hers, but she also uses Durkee's instead of mayonnaise and her grandmother was from Wisconsin and served collards with biscuits instead of cornbread. I do not peel mine, unless Lisa makes me.

Once the tomato is sliced to the desired thickness, spread mayonnaise to taste on both sides of the white bread. (You can make a tomato sandwich on whole wheat bread, but why would you?) Place the tomato slices on the bread to cover and sprinkle generally with salt and black pepper. The fresher and softer the bread, the better. If the whole thing sticks to the roof of your mouth, you have achieved perfection. Just wash it off with a big swig of sweet iced tea and savor the moment.

The tomato sandwich is the lunch time staple at our house in the summer time. I have been known to eat them for lunch every day for weeks at a time. You can brown bag them, too. If you want to do that but aren't allowed to carry a pocket knife—or other sharp objects—at work, simply prepare the bread as you would normally and peel and slice the tomatoes as you would normally. Then pack the bread in one Zip-loc bag and the tomato slices in another and assemble your sandwich at work, when it is time to eat it. You'll have a delicious lunch and your co-workers will be really jealous, because whatever they are having—it won't be as good as what you are having. I guarantee it.

Classic BLT

Right up there with the Classic Tomato Sandwich is the Bacon, Lettuce, and Tomato. It's company good!

3 slices bacon per sandwich

white bread

mayonnaise (or Durkee's)

salt and pepper

fresh crisp iceberg lettuce leaves

First you fry up a mess of bacon and let it drain on paper towels for a couple of minutes while you grease your bread. For this one I toast my bread before spreading it with mayo. (Or Durkee's.) Yes, Lisa prefers it on her BLT, also. She has even brainwashed our son, Jackson, into eating Durkee's on his sandwiches. Peel and slice a tomato or two, depending on how many folks are eating—or how hungry you are, if you are eating alone. Place the tomato on top of one piece of bread and salt and pepper to taste. Criss-cross with bacon slices. Add two or three lettuce leaves. Consume and have a second one.

World Class Grilled Cheese

It is simple. It is easy. It is delicious. It is a great lunch.

2 slices of bread

2 slices of favorite cheese

mayonnaise

1 tbsp butter

Spread mayo on each slice of bread. Place the cheese between the bread slices and toast in a large skillet over medium heat. (About 2 minutes on each side.) After turning the sandwich once, trim half the butter onto the top of the sandwich and then turn over quickly with a spatula. Trim the rest of the butter onto the top of the sandwich. Turn and cook for about a minute on the other side. Serve hot off the stove. (For multiple sandwiches, an electric griddle works great!)

Super Good Fried Ham and Cheese

Everything in the recipe above plus a thick slice of ham.

(The better the ham, the better the sandwich.)

Exactly what you do in the above recipe, except you'll add the ham. You'll think you are eating with Grace and Duck Atkins.

Viennas and Cheese

I ain't making this up y'all. If you want to enjoy a real old fashioned Southern lunch, this is about as old fashioned as it comes. And if it ain't Southern, why do all those "How Southern are you?" tests ask how many Vienna sausages come in a can? (There are seven.) Many is the time that I have sat down on the loading dock at the Porterdale Mill and cracked open a can of Libby's or Hormel Vienna sausages and made a meal of them. They are even better at home because the soda crackers are fresher and less likely to be crumbled. Plus, there is mustard readily available. So here you go.

1 can of premium quality Vienna Sausage

8 or 10 soda crackers (saltines)

6 ounces of extra sharp cheddar cheese

Mustard

Pull the ring tab on top of the can of Viennas and pull back carefully, trying not to spill the juice. Try not to cut your hand, either, if you are a novice. Drain the juice from the can and using a fork—or a rusty Barlow knife—remove the middle sausage. The rest will pour out easier. Cut the cheese into slices or chunks—purely an individual preference—and dab a little mustard onto a small plate for sopping. Enjoy the cheese and sausages with the crackers, dobbing in mustard when you get a notion. Wash down with beverage of your choice. I actually like Dr. Pepper with this meal.

A true Southerner knows how many fish are in a mess and how many Viennas are in a can.

RC Cola and Moon Pie

This is another Southern classic. No. It really is. And it is often called the "working man's lunch." RC Cola originated in Columbus, Georgia and was the first soft drink to be sold in aluminum cans. Moon Pies are out of Chattanooga, Tennessee. Now tell me that ain't a Southern combination if there ever was one!

One ice cold can of Royal Crown Cola.

One chocolate Moon Pie. (Get the Double-Decker if you have a big appetite.)

Tear open the Moon Pie and pop the top on the RC. Alternately bite the cookie and take a swig of the drink to wash the gooey marshmallow crème off the roof of your mouth.

Southerners know that there is nothing unusual about asking, "What kind of Co-Cola do you want?"

First Date Chipped Beef on Toast

Yes, this is the same dish soldiers used to call SOS. (It has something to do with a shingle and that's as graphic as I will get.) But let me give you a little background. On our very first date, I took the lady who would become my lovely wife, Lisa, to Steak and Ale—and in those days, that was as good as it got for an old linthead like me. Things must have gone fairly well because the next week—while her parents were out of town—she invited me over for lunch. I was expecting a really nice romantic meal—something to possibly set the mood for what might follow—and I'm not speaking of dessert. That's Chapter 8. Imagine my surprise—nay, dismay—when she served me SOS. I was quite offended and almost didn't call her back—which would have been fortuitous for her. I did call her back, though, and when I got over being disappointed at not having a romantic lunch, I realized that her chipped beef on toast is delicious. Now I have to beg her for it. The chipped beef dish I mean.

> **1 jar dried beef**
> **½ stick butter**
> **3 tbsp flour**
> **2 ½ cups milk**
> **toasted bread (2 slices per person)**

Cut the beef into small pieces, about ½ x 1 inch. Melt the butter in a skillet, add the beef and stir. After a couple of minutes, slowly add the flour, constantly stirring. Then add about 2 cups of milk and stir. If the dish looks too thick, slowly add a little more milk. Continue to stir and cook until gravy begins to bubble a bit. Serve over toasted bread.

Makes 3-4 servings

Hotdogs a la Huckaby

Now there are all kinds of ways to fix hotdogs. The simplest is to place them under the broiler on the toaster oven and turn them every once in a while until they reach the proper degree of doneness. For me, the blacker the better. My mama used to boil the weenies and I thought they were pretty good. Maybe I just didn't know any better. I like to cook weenies on the grill and, just like under the broiler, a little bit charred is a good thing. A lot charred is better. When I was a student at the University of Georgia, hallowed be thy name, there was an establishment on Baxter Street called Lum's and they specialized in hotdogs steamed in beer. I have never tried that at home because someone from the Baptist church might see me buying beer. But I have had Lum's hotdogs and they were pretty good. And, yes—I have roasted weenies over an open fire on a sharp stick and those are pretty good, too.

But the secret to a good hotdog is not so much in the way they are prepared but more in the quality of the meat and the stuff you put on them. When I crave hotdogs I buy either Oscar Mayer Bun Length, Ball Park Franks or Hebrew National Franks. If I'm shopping alone I get the Oscar Meyer Classic franks. When Lisa has a vote, we get the all beef variety. Once in a great while, I buy Nathan's Famous Franks, when I happen to run across them. And I know these aren't particularly Southern, but there has to be some advantages to having all these Yankees among us. Being introduced to Nathan's hot dogs is one of them.

As for the stuff you put on them—again, I say the more the better. Let me tell you how I dress my dog. I start with finely chopped onions. I love onions and when sweet Vidalias are in season I have been known to just mix chopped onions with mustard and ketchup and eat them with a fork. Now you can turn up your nose if you want to, but don't knock it if you haven't tried it. Mustard and ketchup are a must, of course. The Varsity doesn't refer to hotdogs with just mustard as Yankee dogs for nothing. I like traditional yellow mustard, but some folks swear by brown mustard. Now my son, Jackson, wouldn't think about eating a hotdog without chili. We don't make chili just for hotdogs, but I have a friend whose grandfather does. We use Hormel chili with no beans. I also like sauerkraut on my dogs and once in a great while we might have it on hand. Slaw is good, too and a little melted cheese ain't bad. And the buns need to be very lightly toasted.

So there you have it. Cook up the weenies the way you like them and put as much stuff on them as pleases you and eat them with a side of Bush's Best baked beans and a double handful of Lays potato chips and you'll be set for the afternoon. And I bet after reading this you can't go more than a day without having a hotdog. Hold the onions if you plan on doing some hein' and shein' before the next day!

Fried Spam and Cheese Sandwich

Spam was a staple at my house growing up. We ate Spam for breakfast, from time to time, and, although we seldom ate it for supper, I wouldn't say we never did. But mostly Mama kept Spam on hand to serve as a tasty and filling lunch. The best thing about Spam was that it kept. I mean it kept a long, long time. The next best thing was that it was fun to open. A little metal key was attached to the bottom of the can. You would bend back a tab on the side of the can and insert it into a slot on the key—opening Spam was great preparation for knowing how to put together your children's toys on Christmas Eve—and then you would just turn the key and peel back a strip of the can, all the way around, until the top came off, revealing a covering of what I used to call "meat jelly" on top. Once you scraped that off you were good to go. All you had to do was slice the Spam and eat it—or put it on a sandwich. Instant meal!

You could warm it up in a frying pan if you wanted to, but that was purely optional. There were—and still are—lots of ways to consume Spam. Here is my very favorite.

Two slices of white bread

Mayonnaise

Two slices of Spam

Two hand-cut slices of cheddar cheese

Open the Spam and scrape off the meat jelly. Cut the Spam into ¼ to ½ inch slices and heat it in a frying pan over medium heat. Cook until the edges begin to char. While the Spam is cooking, cut a couple of slices of cheddar cheese—I like extra sharp, but that's purely a personal preference. (Don't ruin a Spam sandwich by using pre-cut sandwich slices. They are too thin.) Spread mayo onto the bread. Top with Spam and cheese and lightly toast in a dry frying pan, just until the cheese begins to melt. Volia! It's 1956 again.

Makes one doggone good sandwich

Saturday Sloppy Joes

My kids were never fond of the Sloppy Joes they were served, from time to time, at school and don't even try to get them to eat one prepared from that canned stuff. But they were smart enough to know that the ones their daddy made from scratch—well, those were fit to eat.

1 lb ground round

2 tbsp cooking oil

4 hamburger buns

2 tbsp butter

1 tbsp mayonnaise

1 medium onion

¼ cup ketchup

¼ cup mustard

2 tbsp Worcestershire sauce

salt and pepper

The first thing you'll do is peel and finely chop the onion and begin to sauté it in the oil, over medium heat. When the onion begins to get translucent, add the ground beef. Constantly chop and stir so that the meat does not clump. While the meat is cooking, spread mayo on one side of each bun and butter on the other.

When the hamburger meat is almost done, carefully drain the grease from the pan. Return the pan to the stove and add the ketchup, mustard, Worcestershire sauce, salt and pepper. Continue to stir, making sure that the meat is well coated. While the meat is finishing up, slide the buns into a preheated oven for just a couple of minutes. You want them warm and soft, not crusty and toasted.

Spoon Sloppy Joe mixture over the buns and serve warm with fries or potato chips and dill pickles. Guaranteed hit!

Makes 4 hefty sandwiches. (You can add another bun or two and make 5 or 6 not so hefty ones.)

Pack 60 Beanie-Weenies

I was a Cub Scout in Pack 60. Walter Pope was my Cubmaster for a while. I think he succeeded Coleman Henry. One of the highlights of the Cub Scout calendar was the annual Beanie-Weenie Banquet in February. I became a big fan of beanie-weenies. Here's how we make them at our house.

1 medium can of Bush's Best baked beans

5 Oscar Mayer beef franks

¼ cup ketchup

¼ cup mustard

1 small onion

1 tbsp cooking oil

Peel and finely chop the onion, then begin to sauté it in the oil. (about 2 minutes) Chop the franks into 1 inch slices and add them to the pan. Stir-fry the franks and onions for another 2-3 minutes. Empty the canned beans into a boiler and add the weenies, onions, ketchup, and mustard and cook over medium heat until warm throughout. Serve with white bread and a side of slaw and pretend you are in the dining hall at Bert Adams Scout Reservation on a Saturday night in February.

Key West Broiled Fish Sandwich

Every chance we get, my lovely wife, Lisa, and I set sail for Mile Marker 0. Whenever we are there, we indulge ourselves by continuing our eternal search for the perfect fish sandwich. This may not be it, but it has to be pretty close. One issue, of course, is what kind of fish to use. Flounder is my favorite. Grouper is great, too. Both are hard to find. Tilapia is a worthy substitute and is readily available in most supermarkets.

4 small filets of your favorite fish

1 tbsp lemon juice

4 tbsp melted butter

salt and pepper

Tabasco sauce

lettuce

4 sandwich rolls

2 tbsp mayonnaise

4 slices fresh tomatoes

Tartar sauce

4 slices Kraft American cheese

Melt the butter in a microwave or in a pan over low heat. Stir in the lemon juice. Wash the fish filets and pat them dry. Sprinkle them on either side with salt and pepper and then brush them on either side with the melted lemon/butter. Cook under a broiler, about five inches from the heat—about 3-4 minutes on either side.

Meanwhile, spread mayo on either side of your favorite sandwich rolls and add a slice of cheese to the underside of the top half. Warm in a toaster oven—or oven—until bread is soft and cheese begins to melt. Remove the roll from the oven and add the fish and top with Tartar sauce, Tabasco, lettuce and tomato. Serve with a big slice of the most tart Kosher dill pickles you can find and your favorite island beverage.

Makes 4 sandwiches

This Little Pig in a Blanket

2 cans of Hormel Vienna Sausage

or

1 package of cocktail weenies

1 can "whomp" biscuits

Open the biscuits by whomping the can on the edge of the kitchen counter. Separate the layers and roll one biscuit around each sausage or weenie, leaving the ends uncovered. Place on a baking sheet, seams down, and bake in a pre-heated oven at 400 until biscuits are done—about 10-12 minutes or so. Heat a can of Bush's Best baked beans and you've got a simple lunch worth saying grace over.

A true Southerner knows that "yore mama 'n' 'em" refers to a person's mother, aunts, neices and all other female acquaintances. "How's yore mama 'n' 'em?" is a perfectly legitimate question in the South.

Boonie Barnes Hamburger Foil Packs

Aubrey (Boonie) Barnes was, for years and years, Scoutmaster of Troop 226 in Porterdale. I don't know how many of these packets he sampled during his career. Believe it or not, they still make a pretty good meal, even when cooked in an indoor oven instead of over hot coals. Best of all, they can be prepared ahead and placed in the oven with no muss and no fuss. If it has been years since you've made these, try it again. They are not just for campouts anymore!

1 ¼ lb lean ground beef

4 small potatoes

2 onions

4 carrots

Worcestershire sauce

salt and pepper

4 lengths of aluminum foil

Form the ground beef into 4 patties. Peel the potatoes and cut into slices. Peel and quarter the onion. Cut each carrot into 4 slices. Arrange the meat and equal portions of the potatoes, onion slices and carrots on the four pieces of foil. Sprinkle with salt, pepper and Worcestershire sauce. Fold the foil over, making a tight package of each. Bake in a preheated oven for 45 minutes and serve.

Makes 4 meals

New Orleans-style Fried Shrimp Po Boy

Nothing is more Southern than New Orleans and nothing soothes the hungry Southern soul better than a Po Boy sandwich. Here's how I make mine—and they are special!

Remoulade Sauce

4 ounces mayonnaise

1 tbsp horseradish

1 tbsp sweet salad cubes

½ tsp salt

½ tsp black pepper

½ tsp red pepper

½ tsp garlic powder

½ tsp Tabasco sauce

2 tbsp lemon juice

Shrimp

6 medium shrimp per sandwich (peeled and deveined)

oil (to cover)

½ cup flour

1 egg

½ cup milk

salt and pepper to taste

shredded lettuce

tomato slices

bread

6 inch loaf of French bread, sliced in half

For the Remoulade sauce, simply combine all the ingredients in a big bowl and stir with a whisk for three minutes. Then refrigerate until needed.

For the shrimp, break the egg into the milk and beat with a whisk for 2-3 minutes. Combine the flour, salt and pepper. Heat the oil to a temperature of 350. Dip the shrimp into the milk-egg mixture, roll them in the flour and place on wax paper for about 5 minutes. Fry shrimp in oil, a few at a time, until done.

Lightly toast the bread. Add the shrimp, lettuce, and tomatoes and top with Roumalade sauce. Add a few dashes of Tabasco if you really want to feel like you are in the Crescent City. Serve with favorite beverage.

Down South Reuben Sandwich

I am well aware that the Reuben is more at home in a New York deli than a Southern kitchen, but if we are going to have to put up with all these Yankees being down here amongst us, we might as well get something out of it, even if it is just a decent sandwich—and trust me--this sandwich is definitely decent. I learned to eat Reuben sandwiches one February, while sitting in the intensive care waiting room at Crawford Long Hospital for a week, waiting for my daddy to die. I wasn't a bit hungry and hadn't eaten in a day or two and a friend brought me a Reuben and made me eat it. It was delicious and I ate one every day for the rest of the week. I became a fan and finally decided to learn how to make them at home. Now you can, too.

2 slices of good deli rye bread per sandwich

2 slices of good corned beef or pastrami

1 slice of provolone cheese

1 tbsp thousand island salad dressing (and/or Dijon mustard)

4 ounces sauerkraut (available in cans or fresh in deli section of most supermarkets)

butter

Put together the sandwich by layering the meat, cheese and sauerkraut, then topping with dressing (or mustard). In a hot frying pan over me-

54

dium heat, toast the sandwich for about a minute on either side, then add butter and cook for another minute on each side. Be careful not to use too much butter as this will make the bread soggy. Remove from skillet and serve hot with a big Kosher pickle.

Maybe those Yankees are on to something after all. Makes one great sandwich!

Southern-Style Buffalo Chicken Sandwich

If we can have a Reuben in a Southern cookbook, I reckon we can have a Buffalo-style sandwich, too. After all, we are getting more and more cosmopolitan every day. (That means that a lot of Yankees are moving in.) Anyway—this sandwich is good.

2 oz bottle Tabasco Sauce

1 stick butter

1 tsp garlic powder

4 boneless chicken breasts

8 slices thick-cut barbecue bread

2 tbsp olive oil

1 tbsp lemon juice

salt and pepper

tomato slices

lettuce

3-4 dill pickle slices per sandwich

1 tbsp ranch or bleu cheese dressing per sandwich

Make the Buffalo sauce by melting a stick of butter in a saucepan over medium heat. Slowly stir in the Tabasco sauce and garlic powder and heat over extremely low heat.

Beat the chicken breasts flat with a kitchen mallet and sauté in olive oil until browned (about five minutes per side). Coat the chicken in Buffalo sauce. Lightly toast the bread and then construct the sandwich by placing the chicken on the bottom slice of toasted bread and topping with lettuce, tomato, dill pickles, and dressing of your choice. Serve with salt-and-vinegar potato chips and Dr. Pepper for a solid Southern lunch.

Makes 4 sandwiches

South Philly Cheese Steak Sandwich

I know. I know. But a couple of pretty prominent Southerners, George Washington and Thomas Jefferson, made big news in Philadelphia back in the day, so why not include a lunch time treat from the City of Brotherly Love. Besides—the two most famous spots for enjoying a classic cheese steak are in South Philly. That would be Pat's and Geno's. Geno won his 15 minutes of fame shortly after 9/11/01 when he began refusing service to anyone who wouldn't try to order in English—and that's a pretty Southern attitude if you think about it. Anyway, here is how I make my Philly Cheese Steak sandwiches.

Oh, yeah. At both Pat's and Geno's, they serve their sandwiches "Whiz with" if you want Cheese Whiz and you just keep your yap shut if you don't. This recipe is Whiz with. If you don't want Cheese Whiz, just leave it off.

16 oz thinly sliced steak

salt and pepper

1 tbsp oil

8 oz cheese (sliced provolone or equivalent amount of

Cheese Whiz spread)

2 medium onions

1 red pepper

1 green pepper

1 tbsp butter

4 6 inch Italian sandwich roll

salt and pepper

Slice about a pound of steak (eye of round is a good cut) as thin as possible and season with salt and pepper. Peel and slice the onions into thin strips. Core and slice the peppers into thin strips. Heat the oil in a non-stick skillet and then stir-fry the steak for 5-7 minutes until brown. Remove steak from skillet and keep warm. Add butter to pan and stir-fry the onions and peppers until tender. Lightly toast the Italian rolls in a warm oven. Build the sandwich by adding the steak, onions, peppers and cheese of choice. Place on baking pan and heat in oven for a minute or two until cheese melts.

Makes 4 sandwiches

What's for Supper?

Entrees

What's for Supper?

Entrees

Supper time! When I was growing up in Porterdale, supper time was the central point of our day. We ate at 6 o'clock because that's when my daddy got to come home from the mill to eat. Actually we ate at 6:05. Mama listened to the radio while she cooked supper—WGFS—The Voice and Choice of the Piedmont Area. WGFS signed off at 6 o'clock every day and Mr. Bill Hoffman, who owned the station, would announce "and as each evening at signoff time, here's Perry Como with the Lord's Prayer." Perry's "Amen" would be followed by Mama's "put the ice in the glasses."

I hated putting the ice in the glasses. My skin still crawls when I think about those old metalic trays with the little levers on top. If you didn't hold them under warm water your skin would stick to the metal ice tray.

By the time I finished the unpleasant task of filling what had once been jelly jars with ice, Daddy's old Buick would be pulling up behind the house and we'd be sitting down to "ask the blessing," which is what we called saying grace. "God is great, God is good . . ." was the standard when it was my turn—or my sister Myron's. My father's blessing of choice was a bit more elegant.

Grace was always short and sweet because time was of the essence—Daddy only got 30 minutes to eat—and there was a lot of conversation to be shared and a lot of good food to eat. We had real discussions about real problems and real triumphs and real events. If the phone happened to ring during the supper hour it went unanswered. If there had been cell phones in those days, there would have been no texting at Homer Huckaby's supper table.

And when I say we ate supper, I mean we really ate a supper. Meat and vegetables and bread every night—fried chicken, fried steak, meatloaf, spaghetti, roast beef, hamburger steak— not to mention mashed potatoes and black-eyed peas and turnip greens and butterbeans and cooked cabbage and . . . wow!

Now you can't set your watch by what time we start, but the Darrell Huckaby family has always sat down to supper together, too—with the television off. And the food has always been pretty good. If you don't believe me—just keep reading.

Porterdale Fried Chicken

If there ever was a go-to dish, this would be it. My mama, Tommie Huckaby, cooked the best fried chicken in the world—period. Don't bother trying to argue the point with me, either. The Huckaby family never left for a trip of more than two hours duration without a shoebox full of her fried chicken along, just in case. After I was grown and out of the house, she still indulged me by fixing her fried chicken for me and my friends and at least once a week she would fix it for supper. When she served it up hot off the stove with black-eyed peas and mashed potatoes and gravy and homemade biscuits--supper just didn't get any better than that.

1 fryer, cut-up

salt

2 cups milk

2 cups plain flour

cooking oil (or Crisco)

Cut up, skin and wash a fryer size chicken. If you could find one that is about 2 ½ pounds you would really be in business. Unfortunately, today's growers try to plump up their chickens 'til they all favor Dolly Parton and the pieces are really too big. Just but the smallest fryer you can find and do your best. Rub the chicken pieces with salt and soak for 20 minutes in sweet milk. (You can use buttermilk if you want buttermilk fried chicken.) Drain the chicken, then dredge in flour. (I mix a little salt into my flour, too.) Heat the oil in a large skillet to a temperature of about 360. Cook with the plumpest part of each piece turned down for about 10-12 minutes. Turn and cover with skillet lid, turning heat down to medium low. Cook another 15-20 minutes, until done. Drain on paper towel and serve. Prepare to be adored by anyone lucky enough to partake.

Serves 4

Eckrich Sausage with Onions and Peppers

I discovered this dish on a camping trip during the summer of 1986 and we have had it for supper about once a month ever since. It is easy and tasty and won't cost you a fortune. And if you can't get Eckrich brand smoked sausage—go ahead and muddle ahead with whatever brand you can come up with.

1 ½ pounds Eckrich brand smoked sausage

2 medium onions

2 green bell peppers

6 yellow squash

½ pound sliced mushrooms

1 tbsp olive oil

salt and pepper

Cut the sausage into 1 inch circles. Peel and cut the onions into eighths. Core the peppers and remove the seeds. Slice into eighths. Peel the squash and cut into ¾ inch circles. Heat the oil in a large skillet and roll the skillet around to coat the bottom. Sautee the onions and peppers for a couple of minutes and then add the remaining ingredients. Sprinkle with salt and pepper to taste. Cook over medium heat for 12-15 minutes until sausage is warm through and the vegetables are tender. Serve with rice and Hawaiian sweet rolls for a great weeknight supper.

Serves 4-6

Southerners know that "y'all" is perfectly good English, and always refers to more than one.

61

Chicken Noodle Casserole

1 whole chicken

1 bag medium noodles

1 small onion, finely chopped

2 celery ribs, chopped

1 stick butter

1 can Cream of Chicken soup

1 can Cream of Mushroom soup

1 cup milk

2 cups shredded cheddar cheese

Boil the chicken in a large pot of water until it is falling off the bone done. This will take about an hour. Remove from water and allow to cool. Remove chicken from the bones. Place the noodles in the leftover broth and water and boil until tender—about 10-12 minutes. Drain in a colander. Melt the butter in a pot and sauté the onions and celery until tender—but not brown. Add the 2 cans of soup and milk to the butter and vegetables. Mix in the chicken and noodles. Pour into a 9x13 casserole dish and sprinkle the cheese over the top. Bake at 325 for about an hour—until the casserole is bubbly and a golden brown.

Makes 6 servings

Every true Southerner knows the difference between a hissy fit and a canniption.

Daddy's Pork Chops and Rice

This is another dish that is delicious and filling and doesn't require a lot of time slaving over the stove.

6 pork chops

2 medium onions

2 tbsp butter

1 tbsp Worcestershire sauce

½ can Campbell's Cream of Mushroom Soup

1 ½ cup Uncle Ben's whole grain brown rice

3 ¼ cups water

salt and pepper

Melt the butter over low heat in a large skillet. Peel onions and slice into 1 inch strips. Brown the pork chops on both sides in butter and season with salt and pepper. Remove pork chops from the skillet and place in a lightly greased 9x13 baking dish and place onion strips on top of the pork chops. Sprinkle the rice over the pork chops and onions. Mix the soup with the water, stirring until soup is dissolved. Add the Worcestershire sauce and pour the mixture into the skillet and stir for about two minutes. Pour the liquid over the pork chops and rice, making sure that all of the rice is covered. Cover the dish with aluminum foil and bake at 350 for about 45 minutes. Remove the foil for the last five minutes.

Feeds 4-6

Chicken Breast on Beef

6 to 8 Boneless, skinless chicken breasts

(1 med. breast per roll)

1 small jar of dried beef

bacon (1/2 slice per breast)

1 can mushroom soup

1 small container of sour cream

Lay the slices of dried beef on bottom of an 8x12 Pyrex dish. Wrap each breast in half slice of bacon and place on dried beef. (place close together) Mix the soup and sour cream together and pour over the chicken. Bake uncovered at 325 degrees for 2 hours, or until done.

Makes 4-6 servings

Butter Baked Chicken

We are talking about a Thursday night supper now—or maybe even a night when one of the kids has a friend over. This isn't your typical Monday or Tuesday supper, in other words—but it is easy enough to be.

8 pieces of chicken (thighs, legs and breast pieces)

1 can Campbell's Cream of Chicken Soup

1 can condensed milk

1 stick butter (thus the name)

½ cup plain flour, salt and pepper

Melt the butter in a casserole dish. Salt and pepper the chicken and roll in the flour. Place in dish and bake at 375 for 30 minutes. Mix the undiluted soup with the milk and stir until well blended. Remove chicken from the oven and turn over. Pour the soup/milk mixture over the chicken and bake for another hour. This goes great with rice and a green vegetable and the "leavings" are perfect for pouring over the rice. *Feeds 4-6*

Country Fried Steak a la Lisa--with Onion Gravy

You just can't get more Southern than country fried steak and my lovely wife, Lisa's, is as good as anybody's. If you are counting your calories or afraid to enjoy biscuits and gravy—or don't like to use the black pepper—well, you might as well cook something out of one of them skinny people's cookbook—but this dish is good, or grits ain't groceries.

4 pieces of cube steak

½ tsp salt

2 tsp black pepper

1 cup all purpose flour

cooking oil

Heat the oil in a large skillet. Mix the salt and pepper with the flour. Dredge the pieces of steak in the flour and fry in about ¼ inch of cooking oil over medium heat until browned on each side. Then reduce heat and cover the pan. Continue to cook about 5-7 minutes longer on each side. Remove the steak from pan and keep warm while making the gravy.

Onion Gravy

The leavings from the cube steak you just cooked

½ onion, thinly sliced

½ cup all purpose flour

1 ½ cup water

Sautee the onions in the steak leavings until brown and soft, then gradually add the flour, stirring constantly. Add water slowly, while stirring, until the gravy reaches desired consistency. Serve immediately, while warm. This is not theologically sound, but I have heard it said that you can lose your salvation if you serve this dish without having homemade biscuits for sopping the onion gravy.

If you prefer smothered steak, simply add the steak back to the pan once the gravy is done and cook for a couple more minutes.

Feeds 4

Chicken Fried Steak

Now this dish is a staple in Texas, but it tastes pretty doggone good in Georgia, too.

4 pieces of cube steak

1 egg

½ cup milk

1 ½ cup flour

salt and pepper

½ cup cooking oil

Break the egg into a bowl. Add the milk and beat well. Mix the flour, salt and pepper together. (Aluminum pie pans are great for this!) Dip each piece of steak in the egg mixture and dredge it in flour to make a thick coating. In a large skillet, heat the oil. Fry up the steak in about ¼ inch of oil. When the steak is well browned on one side, flip it over and brown the other side. Then lower the heat and cover, cooking about 5-7 more minutes on each side. Serve with mashed potatoes and butterbeans and homemade biscuits and you will be celebrated across the land. And don't forget the milk gravy.

Milk Gravy

This goes over the chicken fried steak and the mashed potatoes.

pan drippings from the chicken fried steak

½ cup plain flour

2 cups milk

salt and pepper

Stir the flour into oil over medium-high heat. Slowly add the milk, stirring constantly with a whisk, until the gravy reaches the desired consistency. (Don't fret over it; practice makes perfect.) Add salt and pepper to taste.

Makes 4 servings

Chicken and Dumplings

You just can't get more Southern. This is how our friend Holle Stapp makes them.

1 whole chicken

1 cup self rising flour

¼ cup shortening

1/3 cup milk

1 tsp salt

1 tbsp black pepper

Cover chicken with water and cook until done. This will take about an hour. Let it cool and remove from the bone, tearing or cutting into bite-size pieces. Skim the fat off the chicken broth. Make the dumplings by combining the flour, salt and pepper. Cut in the shortening until the whole thing resembles coarse cornmeal. Add the milk and mix until moistened. Add the chicken to the broth in a large pot and bring to a boil. You will need about 8 cups. Canned broth is acceptable if boiling the chicken didn't make enough.

Drop a heaping tbsp of dough at a time into the dough to make the dumplings. Once all the dumplings have been dropped, cover and reduce heat. Simmer about ten minutes without lifting the top.

Chicken Roll-Ups

2 chicken breasts

1 cup grated cheddar cheese

½ cup more, grated cheese

1 can Campbell's Cream of Chicken/Mushroom Soup

1 can crescent rolls

½ cup milk

Boil the chicken in water until done. This will take about 20-25 minutes, depending. Allow it to cool and then shred into small pieces. Open the crescent rolls. Separate and spread each one out flat. Place a small amount of the chicken and the cheese on each and then roll them up, as if to bake. Mix the soup with ½ cup of milk and pour into the bottom of a lightly greased 9x13 baking dish. Place the roll-ups in the pan, on top of the soup. Sprinkle with the rest of the cheese and bake uncovered at 350 for about 30 minutes.

Feeds 4

Chicken Stuffing Casserole

When my kids come home from college they would rather have this for supper than a T-bone steak.

3 chicken breasts

2 cans Campbell's Cream of Chicken/Mushroom Soup

1 box Stovetop Cornbread Stuffing Mix

2 cups chicken broth

½ stick butter

Boil the chicken in water until done. This will take about 20-25 minutes, depending. Shred the chicken, once it is cooled, and save the broth. Mix the 2 cans of soup with 1 cup of the chicken broth. Melt the butter and mix the melted butter with the stuffing mix. Add 1 can of chicken broth to the stuffing and butter mixture. Spread the chicken out in the bottom of a lightly greased 9x13 inch casserole dish. Pour the soup mixture over the chicken and spread the stuffing mixture on top. Bake for about 30 minutes at 325 until golden brown. Serve with a green vegetable and some fruit salad and you got a supper worth eating.

Makes 6 servings

Pizza Casserole

1 pound ground beef

4 oz jar of Pizza sauce

2 cups shredded mozzorella cheese

2 eggs

1 ½ cup milk

¾ cup Bisquick

Brown the ground beef and drain. Place the meat in the bottom of a lightly greased baking dish. 13x9 works well. Spoon the pizza sauce over the ground beef and add a layer of cheese. Mix the eggs, milk and Bisquick together and pour over the top. Do not stir. Bake at 400 for 30 minutes, until golden brown on top. Yummy!

Monday Night Meatloaf

If you are going to have meatloaf, you might as well have good meatloaf—and this is good. I guarantee it!

> 2 lbs ground chuck
>
> 1 envelope Lipton's Onion Soup Mix
>
> 1 ½ cup plain bread crumbs
>
> 2 eggs
>
> ¾ cup water
>
> 1/3 cup ketchup plus 1/2 cup more for topping

Preheat the oven to 350. Combine all ingredients and shape into a loaf in one large (or 2 small) loaf pans. (If you make two small ones, you can freeze one if you don't need them both. They keep well.) Bake for about 45 minutes, until done, draining any accumulated grease and topping with a bit more ketchup for the last 5 minutes.

Small loaf feeds 4 (If they ain't real hungry)

Any real Southerner knows that "fixin'
to" means "I will get around to it terrect-
ly, but in my own good time."

Huckaby Hamburger Steak

I guarantee you—serve this to your family with a few battered steak fries and a tossed green salad and a can of Le Seuer Early Peas and nobody at your house will go to bed hungry. Or if they do, it will be their own fault. Now honesty compels me to admit that the inspiration for this recipe comes from eating the BP Special at Poss', in Athens, about once a week for four years. Theirs came on a sizzling platter with a baked potato and I will not pretend that I have ever been able to duplicate their perfection—but I've had a lot of satisfying Tuesday night suppers while trying.

2 lbs ground round beef

2 medium onions

4 slices Kraft cheddar cheese

1 tbsp cooking oil

2 tbsp butter

1 tbsp Worcestershire sauce

salt and pepper

Peel and coarsely chop the onions. Using your hands, mold the ground beef into four oblong patties. Pat them down fairly flat so they will cook through. Sprinkle with salt and pepper and Worcestershire sauce. In a large skillet or griddle, heat 1 tbsp of the cooking oil and turn up the heat to high. Place hamburger steaks in the pan and sear on each side for about 2 minutes. Then turn down the heat and cook about 5 more minutes on each side. Meanwhile, in a second skillet, melt the butter and sauté the onions. When the hamburger steaks are almost done, spoon equal amounts of the onions onto each and cover each with a slice of cheese. Cover the pan and allow the cheese to begin to melt. Serve hot. They will be even better if you can find a lady with a gold tooth to set them on the table for you. Trust me on this!

Serves 4

Fried Pork Chops

Remember the scene in *Sweet Home Alabama* when Murphy Brown told Reese Witherspoon's mama to "Go fry something," and she got her lights punched out for it? That's a great scene but, truth be known, we in the South are great at frying stuff. It tastes good, too. It tasted even better when our mamas and grandmamas used to fry everything in lard. Not even I would suggest you do that, but I would suggest you treat your family to these fried pork chops once in a great while.

> **6 pork chops**
>
> **½ to ¾ cup flour**
>
> **salt and pepper**
>
> **½ cup oil**

Heat the oil to a temperature of about 350 degrees. (If you drop a cube of white bread in and it starts to sizzle as soon as it hits the grease, without crisping up immediately, the oil is ready.) Mix salt and pepper with the flour. Dredge the pork chops through the flour and place in hot oil. Brown on one side then turn over. Lower the heat and cover. Fry until done.

Feeds 4

Any Southerner worth his grits understands exactly where you are talking about when you say, "over yonder a piece."

Chicken and Rice Bake

1 cup rice, uncooked

1 can Cream of Mushroom soup, undiluted

1 ¾ cups water

10-12 boneless, skinless chicken thighs

½ tsp salt

¼ tsp black pepper

2 tbsp butter

Pour the rice into a lightly greased 13x9 baking dish and spread it out to cover the bottom of the dish. Combine the soup and the water and pour it over the rice. Place chicken thighs in dish and sprinkle with salt and pepper. Place a tad of butter on each piece of chicken. Cover with foil and bake at 350 for one hour, removing the foil for the last ten minutes.

Beef and Rice Porcupines

This is a favorite of my good friend, Gary Simpson. I am pretty sure he got it from his mama, Lorraine, but it is quick and easy and tastes good.

1 lb ground beef

½ cup raw rice

¼ cup chopped onion

1 tsp salt

¼ tsp black pepper

2 tbsp cooking oil

2 8 oz cans tomato sauce

1 cup water

Mix the beef, rice, onions and seasoning together. Form into small balls and fry in hot oil, turning frequently until light brown on all sides, but not crusty. Add tomato sauce and water. Lower heat and allow to simmer for about 45 minutes.

4 servings

Ham and Potato Casserole

One of the true measures of a good Southern cook is what she—or he—can do with the leftovers. If you had company baked ham on Sunday, this dish is sure to be a treat on Wednesday night—or Monday or Tuesday.

1 lb leftover ham

4 medium potatoes

1 onion

3 tbsp butter

3 tbsp flour

1 ½ cup milk

½ cup grated cheddar cheese

salt and pepper

Peel the potatoes and cut into thin slices. Peel and finely chop the onions. Make a sauce by melting the butter and adding the milk, then slowly stirring in the flour until well mixed. Then butter the bottom of a 13x9 baking dish and line the bottom with a layer of the potatoes. Spread a layer of the chopped onions evenly over the potatoes and then top with a layer of ham. Repeat this process and pour the sauce over the entire concoction, making sure that it soaks all the way down to the bottom layers. Sprinkle with the cheese and cover with foil. Bake for 30 minutes at 350. Remove the foil and bake 30 more minutes.

Makes 4-6 servings

Lisa's Lemon-Pepper Chicken

This has always been a twice-a-month supper staple at our house. The kids love it and so do their friends. I'm right partial to it myself, come to think of it—and it was the first thing my son, Jackson, called home to find out how to fix when he moved into his first apartment at UGA.

2 **whole chicken breasts**

2 **tsp lemon pepper seasoning**

¼ **cup plain flour**

2 **tbsp oil**

2 **tbsp butter**

¼ **cup lemon juice**

Pound the chicken with a meat mallet until flat. That would be somewhere between ¼ and ½ inch thick, according to Lisa. Cut the flattened chicken into strips about an inch wide. Mix the lemon-pepper and flour in a pie pan and roll the chicken in the mixture, coating well. Melt the butteand oil in a skillet, being careful not to burn it. Fry the chicken strips until golden brown—this only takes about 3 minutes per side—and then sprinkle the lemon juice over the chicken. Lower the heat and cook about 10 more minutes until done throughout.

Serves 4 folks

Your family will be on this dish like a duck on a June bug--or like white on rice.

Fried Salmon Patties

Everybody ought to keep a couple of cans of Double-Q salmon in their pantry. When you come home from work late and have to throw supper together and haven't been to the grocery store in several days and don't have anything to fix—this makes a great supper. Serve it with some homemade mashed potatoes and something green—cabbage is pretty good with it. Holy Cow! The South might just rise again, because you'll have a real supper.

1 **can salmon**

1 **egg**

½ **cup bread crumbs (or cracker crumbs)**

1 **tbsp milk**

2 **tbsp oil**

salt and pepper

Drain the salmon and pick out all of the bones and skin. Mix the salmon with the egg, bread crumbs and milk. (You can make cracker crumbs by taking a sleeve of saltines—what we used to call soda crackers before we got so Yankeefied—and crushing them up real fine.) Form into patties—about 3 inches by 2 inches across and ½ to ¾ inch thick—and fry in oil until brown on each side. My brother-in-law, Steve Singley, taught me to pour a little hot pepper sauce over mine before eating. Try it. You'll like it. That may be one reason we serve ours with cabbage and mashed potatoes. The pepper sauce goes real well with the cabbage, too.

Fried Ham Steak

Now if you are looking for easy, this is about as easy as it gets. But it makes a stomp down good supper.

1 fully cooked center-cut ham slice

Unwrap the ham steak from the packaging. Fry the ham about 8-10 minutes on each side. Serve with fried potato rounds, a can of Le Sueur Early Peas and a can of peaches. Laugh if you want to, but when you have three kids that each have to be somewhere in 45 minutes and you are determined that you will all eat supper together—well, you can thank me when you see me. By the way—if you are in a hurry, it is perfectly acceptable to serve canned or frozen biscuits—or crescent rolls, with this meal. You have my blessings.

What's for Supper ?

Vegetables and sides

Suppertime

Vegetables and Sides

When I was coming up, vegetables were a staple on every Southern table at every meal. Every Southerner I knew grew vegetables themselves, or knew someone who did. The fruits of the garden were more abundant in the summer, but we had them in the winter, too—because everybody I knew—and I mean everybody—spent their summer evenings "putting up" food for the winter. We snapped, we shelled, we hulled, we husked—and we froze and we canned and we made jelly and jam and we ate well. Man did we ever eat well.

I haven't planted a garden for a long time, but my in-laws do. I also have a wonderful friend, Ben Evans, to whom this book is dedicated, that sells the best produce anywhere. He and Dolores have been in the produce business for more than thirty years, and theirs is a true family business.

I have done business with Ben for about twenty-five of those thirty years and have watched his sons grow up working at his produce stand and his grandchildren grow up working at his produce stand. I have become close friends with his family and have come to admire Ben more with each passing season.

He gets up every morning before the crack of dawn and drives to the Georgia State Farmers' Market in Forest Park where he picks out the very best—and freshest—fruits and vegetables available. By the time it is good daylight he has spread his wares out on the porch of his market and is ready to visit with his customers as they come in search of good, fresh produce.

Ben has the best the season has to offer, along with a drink box full of Nehi's and RC's and little Co-Colas—with peanuts to pour in 'em. He also has peanuts boiling in a big black pot every day and Southern Gospel music playing overhead. We depend on Ben for our melons in the summer and our pumpkins in the fall and our tree at Christmas—and, of course, our fruits and vegetables year round.

Ben is on Georgia Highway 20, south of Conyers—in the Magnet community—and it will be worth the drive to come and find him. Once you do, you'll become a regular—and if you come on a Saturday morning around ten o'clock—you might just get a chance to visit with your new favorite cookbook author—'cause I am usually right there on the porch.

Fried Collards

You can't get more Southern than collards. They are almost as funda-mental as grits. I'm offering a couple of ways to fix 'em. However it is that you cook collards, please remember that it is a mortal sin to serve collards without having cornbread to soak up the pot liquor. I have a mother-in-law who often serves biscuits with her collards. I can't decide if she does that just to make me mad or if she just doesn't know any better—bless her heart. (Her mama was a Yankee, understand.)

1 large mess of fresh collards

2 quarts water

1 tbsp salt

5 slices bacon

drippings from the bacon

2 tbsp sugar

1 cup water

1 tbsp salt

1 tsp apple cider vinegar

Pick the leaves off the collards and get rid of the stalks and stems. Tear or chop the collards into small pieces. Wash the collard greens well and soak them in salt water for about 10 minutes, then place them in a colander and wash them again, thoroughly. You might even want to wash them a third time.

Fry the bacon in a large Dutch oven or similar pot, saving the drip-pings. Crumble up the bacon and set it aside. Place the collards in the hot bacon drippings and stir-fry them for about 5 minutes. When the collards have cooked down a little, add about a cup of water and the vinegar, salt and sugar. Cover the pot and turn the heat down. Simmer for about 20 minutes, until collards are a dark green.

Remove them to a serving dish and sprinkle the bacon over them. The bacon is purely optional, understand, but the pepper sauce and corn-bread is as mandatory as it gets!

Classic Collards

2 qts water

¼ lb fatback or salt pork

1 tsp sugar

1 large mess of fresh collards

salt and pepper

Pour the water into a large pot. Add a tsp or so of salt and one of sugar, along with the fatback. Cover and bring to a boil. Keep the covered pot at a low boil for about 30 minutes. Prepare the collards just as you did for the above recipe. Add the collards and a little more salt and black pepper to the pot and simmer for two hours, until tender. Serve with pork and sweet potatoes and don't forget the cornbread.

Southern-style Turnip Greens

My mama used to chide me not to "turnip my nose at the greens." She always promised me that a day would come when I would give anything for a mess of her turnip greens and, as usual, she was absolutely right. Here's how she cooked hers, as near as I can remember.

1 large mess of turnip greens

½ pound fatback, sliced

2 cups water

1 cup finely chopped onion

½ tsp pepper

½ tsp salt

1 tsp sugar

Wash the turnip greens and pick away the stems and stalks. Chop or tear the leaves into small pieces and wash again. Slightly brown the fatback in a skillet and pour meat and drippings into a large pot. Add the water, turnip greens, onion and other ingredients. Cover the pot and bring to a boil. Reduce the heat and allow to simmer for 45 minutes to an hour—until the greens are tender. And yes, cornbread is just as essential to enjoying turnip greens as it is collards.

Black-Eyed Peas

Another Southern staple. And although my recipe is for black-eyed peas, field peas and Crowder peas and purple hull peas and all their relatives and derivatives can be prepared in the same manner.

1 lb peas

2 strips bacon (or fatback)

3-4 cups water

1 small onion

1 tsp sugar

1 tsp salt

If you are using dried black-eyed peas, reconstitute them overnight according to the direction on the package. Peel and finely chop the onion. Begin to cook the bacon over low heat. When it begins to become limp, remove it from the pan. Add the peas and the bacon to a boiler and cover with water. Add the onions, salt and sugar and bring to a boil. Lower the heat and simmer for about 40-50 minutes until peas are tender, but not mushy. Drain and serve.

Hoppin' John

You are getting seriously Southern when you tackle this dish. Let me know how it comes out—or better yet, call me to your supper table!

1 pound dried black-eyed peas, reconstituted

6 cups water

1 small ham hock (or a ham bone with meat)

2 medium onions, divided

1 tsp minced garlic, divided

1 bay leaf

1 cup rice

1 can diced tomatoes

1 green bell pepper, chopped

3 stalks celery, chopped

2 tsp Cajun seasoning

¼ tsp black pepper

½ tsp salt

In a large pot, combine the black-eyed peas with the ham hock and cover with about 6 cups of water. Peel one of the onions and cut it in half and toss it in the pot. Add the garlic and the bay leave and bring everything to a boil. Lower the heat and simmer for an hour to 90 minutes. You want the peas to be tender, but not mushy. Remove the peas and ham hocks and drain the pot. Dice the meat and set aside.

Add 2 ½ cups fresh water and a tsp of salt and bring to a boil. Add the rice, cover, and lower the heat. Simmer for about 15 minutes.

Peel and finely chop the remaining onion. Add it and all other ingredients to the rice. Cook about 10 more minutes and serve up piping hot.

Fried Peas

I have seen my mama make a meal of this dish—if you can call it a dish. It ain't particularly healthy, but it is good eatin'.

> **2 cups cold leftover peas**
>
> **½ cup flour**
>
> **1 tbsp bacon grease**
>
> **salt and pepper**
>
> **¼ cup oil**

Add the flour and bacon grease to the cold peas. Mix well and mash the peas using a wooden spoon. Mold into cakes. Sprinkle liberally with salt and pepper and fry in hot oil, about 3-5 minutes per side. They go good with a chunk of Vidalia onion.

Tommie Huckaby's Double-Cut Corn Off the Cob

> **6 ears fresh sweet corn**
>
> **2 tbsp butter**
>
> **¼- ½ cup water**
>
> **salt and pepper**

The secret to this dish is picking out good tender ears of sweet corn. The next part of the secret is how you cut and scrape the corn. Now you must understand—next to her fried chicken, this was my very favorite thing my mama cooked—ever! And I won't pretend that I have mastered it. Mine is not as good as hers, in other words—but it ain't bad.

Shuck the corn and remove the silks, using a stiff brush to make sure they are all gone. Using a sharp knife, cut the tips of the corn into a large bowl. Just the tips. This is important. Next, cut the corn again, this time down closer to the cob. Now you will hold the knife perpendicular to the cob and scrape the "milk" off the corn, into the bowl.

Transfer the corn to a large skillet and add the butter, water and salt and pepper. Cook over low heat until corn is cooked through—about 15 minutes. Watch closely and if the corn begins to run dry add more water.

Makes 4-6 servings

Every Night Squash and Onions

6-8 yellow squash

1 medium onion

½ cup water

2 tbsp butter

salt and pepper to taste

Peel the squash, using a vegetable peeler. Cut it into ¼ to ½ inch slices. Peel the onion and cut into eighths, lengthwise. Add the squash to a frying pan with the water and boil until softened—about 15 minutes. Add the butter and sauté another five minutes. Add salt and pepper to taste.

Makes 4 servings

Fried Okra

Simply put, this is just as good as it gets!

> **2 cups okra, cut up**
> **¾ cup Bisquick**
> **¼ cup cornmeal**
> **2 tbsp milk**
> **salt and pepper**
> **1 inch of oil**

Wash the okra and cut into ½ inch slices. Discard the tops. Put milk in a small bowl and add okra, stirring to soak. Combine the Bisquick, cornmeal and salt and pepper. Heat an inch of oil in a medium skillet. Dredge the okra in the mixture and fry over medium heat until crisp— about 12-15 minutes per batch. Drain on paper towels.

Serves 4

Fried Green Tomatoes

You don't have to go to the Whistle Stop Café to get fried green tomatoes, and even though they have become a trendy "nouveau Southern" thing these days—this is the way my mama fixed them back when they were just something good to eat.

> **3 green tomatoes**
> **¼ cup flour**
> **½ cup cornmeal**

¼ cup milk

2 eggs

salt and pepper

1 inch of oil

Cut the unpeeled tomatoes into 1/3 inch slices. Sprinkle them liberally with salt and pepper and let stand for about 10 minutes. Mix the milk and eggs and beat well. Combine the flour and cornmeal. Dip the tomatoes in the egg mixture and dredge in the cornmeal mixture. Fry in an inch of oil over medium heat until brown—about 5 minutes per side.

Makes 4-6 servings

Pinto Beans

Now let me tell you something, Hoss. You cook up a pot of pintos and serve them up with a chunk or two of Vidalia onion, a hunk of cornbread and maybe some sweet tomato chow-chow and, son—you've got supper!

1 lb dry pinto beans, reconstituted

2 qts water

2 tbsp butter

4 oz salt pork, salt and pepper

You will need to soak the pintos in water overnight. The instructions will be on the package. When it is time to cook them, drain off the beans. Put a couple quarts of water in a big pot and add 1 tsp salt, a little black pepper, the butter and the salt pork. Next add the beans and bring to a boil. Reduce the heat and allow the beans to simmer for about 90 minutes to 2 hours until tender but not mushy. They will be better than snuff and not half as dusty.

Makes 6 servings

Green Beans with New Potatoes

2-3 lbs fresh green beans

4 slices bacon

1 medium onion

6 small new red potatoes

1 cup chicken broth

3-4 cups water

1 tbsp butter

salt and pepper

String the beans and break into pieces—about an inch-and-a-half long. Wash the beans and drain. Peel and chop the onion. Cut the bacon slices into quarters. In a large pot, sauté the bacon and onions in butter until the bacon is getting limp, not crisp, and the onions are becoming tender. Add the beans to the pot. Add the chicken broth and enough water to cover the beans. Bring to a boil and then lower the heat so the beans will simmer. Add the potatoes and cover. Continue cooking until the potatoes are tender but not coming apart.

Serves 4-6

Better Be Worth the Trouble Butter Beans

We're talking Deep South, y'all!

1 lb fresh lima beans (or reconstituted dried beans)

1 small onion, finely chopped

2 slices bacon (or 1 ham hock)

1 tsp salt

1 tsp black pepper

1 tbsp butter

Rinse the beans well under cold running water. Pour the beans into a large pot and cover with water. Bring to a boil and allow the beans to boil for about 5 minutes. Remove the beans from the heat and let them stand for about 45 minutes. Drain the beans and set aside. Now, in the same pot, sauté the onions and bacon in cooking oil until the onions are tender. Return the beans to the pot and cover with water. Add salt and pepper to taste. Bring the whole thing to a boil and then reduce the heat and allow the beans to simmer for another hour or so, until done.

Makes 6 delicious servings

Pressure Cooker Green Beans

1 lb fresh green beans

1 cup chicken broth

Water to cover

1 tbsp bacon grease (or butter)

salt and pepper

Wash and string the fresh green beans and break into pieces. Place the beans in the pressure cooker. Add the chicken broth and enough water to cover the beans. Add the bacon grease (or butter, if you have Yankee blood and are squeamish about keeping bacon grease on hand) as well as a little salt and pepper. Lock down the pressure cooker and cook about 30 minutes.

Makes 6 servings

Bitzi's Pressure Cooker Butter Peas

2 cups fresh butter peas

water to cover

1 tbsp butter

salt and pepper

Put the whole shooting match in a pressure cooker. Lock down and cook for about 15 minutes over medium heat.

Makes 4-6 servings

Fried Squash

If God can cause it to grow, we in the South can batter and fry it. Don't knock it if you ain't done et some yet!

8 yellow squash

1 egg

½ cup milk

1 cup flour or bisquick

salt and pepper

1 inch of oil

Peel the squash and cut into ¼ inch thick slices. Beat the egg and milk together. Combine the flour, salt and pepper in a pie pan. Dip the squash in the egg mixture and dredge in the flour mixture. Fry on each side until golden brown—about 5 minutes per side. Drain on paper towel and serve up hot.

Makes 4 servings

Everyday Boiled Cabbage

½ head cabbage, shredded

1 cup of water

2 tbsp butter

salt and pepper

Put all the ingredients in a medium pot. Cover and bring to a boil Lower heat and simmer until cabbage is tender—about 30 minutes.

Squash Casserole

2 cups squash

¼ cup finely chopped onion

1 egg, slightly beaten

½ stick butter

1 cup crushed crackers (saltines or Ritz)

1 cup shredded cheese

Boil the squash and onion together until tender. Pour into a colander to drain the liquid. Put the squash and onions back into boiler. Add the egg, butter, crackers, cheese, salt & pepper to taste. Mash with potato masher until smooth and pour into a casserole dish. Top with buttered crackers. Bake at 350 for about 30 minutes or until done.

Makes 6 servings

Corn on the Cob

4-6 ears fresh corn

water to cover

1 tsp salt

2 tbsp butter

Shuck and silk the corn just before cooking it. If you can also pull it just before cooking it, that's even better. We are looking for fresh corn, in other words. Fill a large pot about 2/3 full of cold water. Add the salt and butter and bring to a rolling boil. Carefully add the ears of corn. Cover and let boil for about 7 minutes. Remove from the heat and let stand another 3 minutes. Remove from water and serve.

Baked Apples a la Lisa

This is a wonderful side dish, especially in the fall when Ben Evans gets those good fresh apples from the North Georgia Mountains.

4 medium baking apples

4 tbsp butter

4 tbsp brown sugar

1 tsp cinnamon

Core the apples. Mix the cinnamon and brown sugar. Place the apples in a small baking dish and stuff each with 1 tbsp of butter and ¼ of the sugar/cinnamon mixture. Bake uncovered at 350 for about 45 minutes.

Makes 4 servings

Baked Vidalia Onions

If Vidalia onions aren't available, just wait until the next summer to make this recipe.

4 large Vidalia onions

4 tbsp butter

4 beef bouillon cubes

salt and pepper

Peel each onion and cut out the center core. Insert a bouillon cube into the core of each onion. Stuff each onion with a tablespoon of butter and sprinkle salt and pepper over the top. Wrap each onion individually in aluminum foil and bake at 350 for about an hour.

Canned Corn Casserole

This is Lorie Scroggs's recipe and if Lorie Scroggs puts her name on it, you can count on it being worth eatin'!

1 can creamed corn

1 can whole kernel corn

16 oz sour cream

1 stick butter

1 box Jiffy corn muffin mix

2 eggs (beaten)

Melt the butter in a 13x9 baking dish. Add the two cans of corn, the sour cream and the eggs, and a touch of salt, to taste. Mix everything well. Now add the muffin mix and mix well. Bake at 350 for about an hour.

Makes 6 servings

Baked Sweet Potatoes

Baked sweet potatoes have long been a standard for Southern suppers. My buddy Gary says that his grandpa used to eat one every day. We don't have them quite that often, but we do eat them a lot—year round. Here are three ways to make the perfect sweet potato. Feel free to experiment and pick the one you like best.

Method A

Choose medium-sized sweet potatoes and scrub them well under running water. Wrap immediately in aluminum foil and place in a preheated oven. Bake at 350 for 2 hours. That's it.

Method B

Choose medium-sized sweet potatoes and scrub them under running water. Cover a cookie sheet with foil and place on the bottom rack of an oven which you have preheated to 450. Place the sweet potatoes on the rack immediately above the cookie sheet—not on the cookie sheet. After 20 minutes turn the oven temperature down to 350 and continue cooking for another hour.

Method C

Place the sweet potatoes on a baking sheet and place in a preheated oven. Bake at 400 for 75-90 minutes, depending on the size.

So see? You can't go wrong. Just bust them open and fill them up with butter and maybe a little brown sugar and/or cinnamon.

Mashed Potatoes

You can have these with fried chicken, salmon, pork chops—shoot fire! You can have mashed potatoes with just about anything. There are as many recipes as there are cooks. Some like to add a little garlic, some like to add a little cheese. Some like to leave a little of the skin on, other like to make sure all the skin is off and, to be perfectly honest—I mix it up a little bit. But this is how I cook my traditional mashed potatoes. You feel free to experiment.

6 medium russet potatoes

½ cup milk

4 tbsp butter

¾ tsp salt

pepper to taste

Peel the potatoes (if you'd like) and cut into one inch cubes. Place the potatoes in a boiler, cover with water and boil for about 30 minutes. Drain the water and add the milk, butter, salt and pepper. Mash until the potatoes are light and fluffy. That's it. Doing much of anything else will just make you mess up. Now if you want creamed potatoes, add a lot more milk.

Lisa's fancier version: Melt butter in saucepan and saute 1/2 thinly sliced small onion until light brown, add this with 1/2 cup chicken broth, and use half and half instead of milk and butter above. Tastes delicious, even without gravy.

Makes 6 servings

Special Fries

3 medium potatoes

1 cup milk

1 egg

½ cup cornmeal mix

1 tsp Lawry's Seasoning Salt

1 inch oil

black pepper

Scrub the potatoes and peel them, leaving a few strips of the peelings intact. Cut each potato in half lengthwise and then cut each half in thirds, lengthwise. Mix the milk and egg and beat until well blended. Mix the cornmeal mix and Lawry's together and place in a plastic bag. Dip the potatoes in the egg mixture and drop them in the plastic bag. Shake the bag until the potatoes are well coated. Fry in an inch of hot oil until done. Drain on paper towel and sprinkle with black pepper.

Fried Potato Rounds

3 medium potatoes

1 inch oil

salt and pepper

Scrub and peel the potatoes and slice crossways into ¼ inch circles. Fry in hot oil until done. Drain on paper towels and sprinkle with salt and pepper.

Black Skillet Southern Cornbread

There are lots and lots of ways to make cornbread. Some folks like to make it thick and fluffy, almost like cake. Some people put sugar in it and others add jalapenos and others add cracklings. Some people even put sugar in theirs, put they should be deported. This is how I cook cornbread—at least twice a week--in the black skillet Lisa and I set up housekeeping in.

1 cup cornmeal mix

1 egg

1 cup buttermilk (minus a little bit)

1 tbsp Crisco

1 tbsp melted butter

pinch of salt

Preheat the oven to 425. Place a tbsp of Crisco in the skillet and let the skillet heat up with the oven. Pour the cornmeal mix into a bowl and break the egg into it. When the Crisco is melted, carefully remove the black skillet from the oven (use a mitt!). Roll the skillet around to evenly coat the bottom of the pan and pour the extra oil into the corn-meal mix. Melt the butter in the microwave (takes about 20 seconds) and pour it into the mix, too. Beat the egg into the mix and then slowly pour the buttermilk into the mixture. Pour about half and mix well and then pour a little more and a little more. You will know when the consistency is right and you won't use quite all the buttermilk. Beat until smooth and pour into hot skillet. Bake 22 minutes or until top is golden brown. Remove from oven and turn over onto a serving plate, using a spatula to slide the cornbread out of the pan. You might want to fix two and, yes—at our house cornbread is too a side!

Macaroni and Cheese

Karen Carter, who used to be Harry Dawg's mama, makes the best macaroni and cheese I have ever had, and she has been gracious enough to share her recipe with the world, or at least the part of it lucky enough to have a copy of this book.

8 oz macaroni noodles

1 stick butter

2 eggs

2 cups grated sharp cheddar cheese

dry mustard - couple of shakes

salt - couple of shakes

pepper - little shake

milk

Boil the macaroni, according to the instructions on the package. Drain and add butter, cheese, eggs and spices. You can mix this all right in the pot. Then put it all in a big casserole dish and pour just enough milk to make it a little bit soupy. Top off with a little bit of leftover cheese and bake at 375 for 40-45 minutes, until slightly brown on top.

If it is good enough for Harry Dawg, it's good enough for you!

Makes 8 servings

Scuppernong Jelly

Every Southerner worth his spit knows that when you sit down to eat a good home cooked meal you need to have certain condiments on the table. I ain't talking about just salt and pepper and ketchup and such. I am talking about green tomato chow-chow to go with your beans and stewed tomatoes to go with your peas and pear relish to go with just about anything. And, of course, you need some good preserves or jelly to go with those homemade biscuits. Of all the jellies there are, I think scuppernong is the best—and the most Southern. And of all the scuppernong jelly I have ever tasted, Mary Anne Gordon's is the best.

That makes sense, of course, because Mary Anne is as Southern as they come. Her maiden name was Carroll and her people settled Carrollton, Georgia. Mary Anne's mama, Margaret, once told me that when she was in high school in Carrollton a Yankee moved to town and was giving everybody so much trouble that they tied him to a desk and set him on fire. Now I don't recommend that—but I do recommend that you try this jelly. Mary Anne had this to say.

"Of all the jellies and preserves I make, scuppernong is, by far, my favorite. It takes a little more time than some of the others, but it is well worth the effort. For my family, the sweet and earthy smell of scuppernong jelly on the stove makes it official that the heat and humidity of summer have passed, and that autumn has arrived."

3 pounds scuppernongs or muscadines

½ cup water

7 cups sugar

1 pouch Certo liquid pectin

½ tsp butter (to prevent foaming)

Wash the grapes and pick off any stems. Place the grapes in a large Dutch oven with ½ cup water. Bring to a boil, and then reduce heat. Cover, and simmer for 10 minutes.

Place a fruit sieve or fine strainer over a large mixing bowl. Carefully pour small patches of cooked grapes into sieve or strainer. Using a wooden pestle or heavy wooden spoon, mash grapes to extract juice. When no more juice can be extracted, discard grape skins. Continue until all grapes have been pressed. Including the ½ cup water used when cooking the grapes, you should have four cups of juice. If you are short, you may add just enough water to make exactly four cups.

Combine juice, sugar and butter in the large Dutch oven. Cook on high, stirring constantly with wooden spoon. Bring mixture to a full rolling boil (one that does not stop bubbling when stirred). Add pouch of pectin as quickly as possible. Return to full rolling boil, stirring constantly, for exactly one minute. Remove pot from heat.

Ladle immediately into canning jars, leaving 1/8 inch space. Wipe all rims and threads with wet cloth to remove any spilled jelly. Place lids on jars, and then tightly screw jar bands. Invert jars for 10 minutes to seal.

Some additional notes: This recipe makes approximately seven cups of jelly. Jars and rims that have been washed can be reused, but lids can never be reused. Never ladle boiling liquid into cool jars, as they may break. Keep jars hot by placing them on the warming cycle of the dishwasher or by keeping them in a large pot full of very hot water. Also keep lids and rims in pans of hot water while preparing jelly. Once jar rims have been tightened and jars have been inverted for 10 minutes, never attempt to again tighten bands. This will break the seal of the jar. Last but not least, jelly making is an exact science. Make sure to measure all ingredients and time all cooking very carefully.

There you have it! Do your part to preserve Southern culture and learn to make jelly—Mary Anne's way.

Sweet Tomato Relish

Ain't nothin' better with crowder peas.

1 qt fresh tomatoes, cooked down

2 Vidalia onions, finely chopped

3 sweet peppers, chopped

2 hot finger peppers, finely sliced (seeds removed)

2 cups sugar

1 cup vinegar

1 clove

1 tsp salt

Mix everything in a big pot and bring to a boil. Reduce heat and allow to simmer all afternoon—4 or 5 hours. Your kitchen will never have smelled better. Spoon the relish into sterilized jars and seal. Place in a boiling water bath for 15 minutes.

Granny Huckaby's Pear Relish

2 qts fresh pears, ground

2 lbs Vidalia onions, peeled and ground

3 red bell peppers, seeded and ground

3 green bell peppers, seeded and ground

1 yellow bell pepper, seeded and ground

1 hot green pepper, seeded and ground

2 tbsp salt

1 tbsp turmeric

2 cups sugar

1 tsp celery seed

3 tbsp prepared mustard

4 tbsp flour

1 cup vinegar

2 more cups vinegar

Mix the pears, onions and all the peppers in a large glass bowl and set aside. Mix the next 7 ingredients together in a boiler and cook until it thickens up, stirring constantly. Add the rest of the vinegar and stir. Place the pears, peppers and onions in a large pot and pour the boiling mixture over the pears. Bring this to a boil and let boil for 15 minutes, stirring constantly as the vegetables have a tendency to stick. Spoon relish into sterilized jars and seal. Place jars in a boiling bath for about 15 minutes and then set dry off the jars and set them in the pantry for a couple of months, to mellow.

Green Tomato Chow Chow

1 gal green tomatoes, chopped

1 cabbage, chopped

6 green bell peppers, chopped

4 hot finger peppers, chopped (take out the seeds)

1 cup onion, chopped

3 cups vinegar

2 cups sugar

2 tbsp salt

Chop all the vegetables and set aside. Combine the vinegar, sugar and salt in a large pan and bring to a boil. Add the vegetables to the vinegar mixture and lower the heat. Allow to simmer for about 20 minutes, stirring often. Pour into sterilized pint jars and seal. Place in a boiling water bath for 20 minutes. Allow to mellow for a few weeks.

Sweet Tea

In the South of my boyhood, nobody ever asked "Sweet or unsweet?" when it came to iced tea. In fact, nobody even asked if you wanted iced tea. You just got it. Period. That's what people drank with their supper. Nowadays people are messing with our sweet tea. They are trying to flavor it and make it with diet sweeteners and all sorts of nonsense. Well, it's time to take a stand. Real Southerners drink sweet tea at supper and this is how we make ours.

2 family sized tea bags (Tetley or Luzianne)

1 qt boiling water

1 ½ cup sugar

1 qt cold water

Fill a kettle with water and put it on to boil. Pour the sugar into the bottom of a two quart pitcher. When the water begins to bowl, add two family sized tea bags and allow to steep for 10 minutes. Pour the hot tea over the sugar. Use a spoon to squeeze the sides of the tea bags. Stir the mixture until the sugar is dissolved and add a quart of cold water. Stir again and allow to sit for 5-10 minutes before serving over ice—lots of ice. There is nothing worse than trying to drink a glass of what is supposed to be iced tea with one or two ice cubes floating around in the glass.

Its a great day

for a cookout!

Time for a Cookout

Ernie Banks, the Hall of Fame ballplayer that spent his entire career with the Chicago Cubs, became famous for his expression, "It's a great day! Let's play two." If you are younger than 50 get an old person to explain the term double-header to you. But the thing was, Ernie Banks loved baseball so much that, to him, any day was a great day to play two.

I'm that way about cooking out. It may be hot as blue blazes outside or I may have to scrape ice off the grill or the fish grease might have to thaw out before we can heat it up—but no matter the weather, to me, any day is a great day for a cookout. And some of my favorite recipes are for those things that I cook in the great outdoors—or at least on the back deck.

Now honesty compels me to admit that my talents as an outdoor chef don't compare to those of the great Bill Travis of Covington. If it swims or crawls or runs or hops or flies, Doc can clean it and cook it up and make it taste good. But I don't do bad for an old linthead—and I have gotten a few of my friends to share one or two of their culinary secrets with me, too.

The bottom line—there is stuff in here you'll like. I guarantee it! Unless you are as fanatical about cooking out as I am, you might want to start this section on a pretty day, because I know you are going to want to get outside and fire up the grill as soon as you start turning these pages.

Basic Grilled Steak

We didn't have a whole lot of money when I was coming up in Porterdale, but about once a month—always on a Saturday night—Daddy would splurge and we would have steaks for supper. Those T-bone steaks sizzling on the grill always made my mouth water. I loved the way they smelled and I loved the way they sounded and, most of all, I loved the way they tasted. To my daddy the T-bone was the King of Steaks. As I have grown older I have grown more partial to the Ribeye--and if you don't think Ribeye should be capitalized, you haven't had one that I have cooked. My kids are a little bit partial to the sirloin strip. Whatever your poison, if you pick up a good cut of meat, season it up well and cook it just right over hot charcoal—or on a gas grill if you must—you'll know what good eatin' is all about.

The key, of course, is a hot fire. If you are cooking on a gas grill, make sure that your grates are well cleaned and well oiled, so that the meat doesn't stick. Allow the grill to heat up before placing the steaks on the grill and keep a close watch so that the meat isn't seared by the flare-ups that occur when the fat drops down on the grill.

If you use charcoal, don't be impatient. Allow the coals to be completely covered with gray ash before you put the steaks on and don't use too much lighter fluid. If you do, the steaks make actually pick up the taste a bit. Also, take the steaks out of the refrigerator and allow them to reach room temperature before getting started.

Ribeye ala Darrell

It all starts with the steak, so pick out a good one that is about 3-quarters to an inch thick and well marbled. Make up the marinade and let them steep for about 30 minutes at room temperature. Build a charcoal fire and light it and let it get hot while the steaks are marinating. Make sure all the fixings are about ready when you put the steaks on the grill so you can serve them up good and hot. And once you perfect the cooking of the recipe, give me about an hour's notice so I can get there to see how you did.

4   10-12 oz Ribeye steaks, well marbled

4 tbsp butter

4 tsp lemon juice

4 tbsp Worcestershire sauce

garlic salt

sea salt and coarsely ground black pepper

Prepare the marinade by melting the butter and blending in the next 4 ingredients. Sprinkle the steaks with salt, pepper and garlic salt. Place the steaks in a covered pan and cover with marinade. Let sit at room temperature for about half an hour, while the fire is getting hot.

Place steaks on clean, hot, well-oiled grill top over hot coals. (Pam for the Grill works great.) After about 90 seconds, turn the steaks about 90 degrees to make the classic grill marks. Flip the steaks over after 5 to 7 minutes, depending on desired doneness. Use tongs to flip steaks, not a fork. Keep in mind that the steaks keep cooking after you remove them from the heat. Also keep in mind that if a steak is too rare you can put it back on the fire. If it is too done you cannot uncook it.

Lime Marinated Shrimp

If you find yourself hungry for a little island flavor, try this recipe. They go well as an accompaniment to the steaks or as an appetizer or as a stand-alone entrée. They are quick and easy and, best of all, delicious.

2 lbs fresh large shrimp, peeled and deveined

½ cup olive oil

½ cup fresh lime juice

2 green onions, finely chopped

¼ tsp minced garlic

2 tbsp brown sugar

¼ cup soy sauce

12 wooden skewers

Carefully heat the oil over medium-low heat, adding the brown sugar and allowing it to melt. Add the onions and let them sauté for a couple of minutes and then remove from heat and add the other ingredients. Peel and devein the shrimp and place in a large bag with the marinade. Allow to marinate for at least six hours. Overnight is better.

Soak the skewers in water for at least thirty minutes prior to using. Thread the shrimp onto the skewers—about five shrimp to each. Grill about 2-3 minutes per side over medium heat, being careful not to overcook.

Makes 6 servings

Low Country Boil

This is my specialty and my very favorite thing to cook outside for a crowd. You may vary the ingredients to suit your taste and the availability and price of the ingredients. Honesty compels me to admit that the only alteration we ever make is that sometimes we have crab legs and sometimes we don't. Technically you can cook this in the house— but it's more fun to cook it outside on a gas cooker.

Obviously you will vary the amounts of the ingredients to suit the size of the crowd you will feed, but I will say that no matter how many folks we have or how much we cook, there is never anything left. The most fun of the whole event is covering the table with newspaper and pouring the feast out for all to enjoy. And there is no need for serving dishes. Folks can use the boarding house reach and serve their plates from the table. We usually do use plates because it seems so much more civilized.

1 really big pot—with a lid

3-4 lbs large shrimp, shell on

6-8 lbs snow crab clusters

2 dozen small red potatoes

4 medium onions

3-4 lbs smoked sausage (Eckrich brand is best.)

8-10 ears of fresh corn, broken in half

4 lemons

1 clove minced garlic

1 package McCormick Shrimp and Crab Boil seasoning

½ cup apple cider vinegar

salt

1 lb butter, melted and drawn

Prepare all the food first and then you will have more time to socialize while the food cooks. You can provide your own definition of socialize. Wash the shrimp and crab legs. Husk and silk the corn and break (or cut if you must) the ears in half. Cut the sausage into 2 inch lengths. Cut the lemons in half. Measure out the vinegar and the garlic and peel the onions. Cut them in half if they are large. Scrub the potatoes.

What you'll do . . .

Fill a large pot 2/3 full of water and add about a tablespoon of salt. Cover and bring to a rolling boil. Only when the pot is boiling, add the onions and potatoes. Cover and cook 20 minutes. Add the crab boil, vinegar, and garlic. Cover and cook 5 minutes. Add the sausage and crab legs. Cover and cook 10 minutes. Add the corn. Cover and cook 10 minutes. (Now would be a good time to melt the butter and skim the fat off the top.) Add the shrimp and immediately turn off the fire or remove pot from heat. Cover and let sit 5 minutes. Drain the water, being careful not to let the steam burn you and—just as importantly— not to lose any of the food.

Once the water is drained, pour out the feast onto a large table that you have covered with several layers of newspaper. Serve with cocktail sauce and clarified butter. Coleslaw makes a good accompaniment. Say Grace and dig in! It is every man for himself—or woman.

Serves 6—10

Easy Cocktail Sauce

½ cup ketchup or chili sauce

1-2 tbsp horseradish

1 tbsp lemon juice

¼ tsp Tabasco sauce

1 tsp worcestershire sauce

Mix well ahead of time and refrigerate. Overnight allows flavors to meld. Experiment to get it to taste just right!

Smoked Boston Butt

There are few things better than barbecue. There are lots of ways to make barbecue. I have been to Texas and I know what they call barbecue in Texas and I generally respect the opinions of Texans. All of that aside, if it don't involve the south end of a north bound hog—it ain't barbecue. Now I am partial to hams and I like shoulders, but one of the easiest—and best—ways to enjoy pork is by smoking a Boston butt on a simple water and charcoal smoker.

5-6 pound Boston butt

2 tbsp salt

1 tbsp black pepper

1 tsp red pepper

2 tsp garlic powder

2 tsp onion powder

2 tsp dry mustard

2 cups apple juice

Fill the charcoal pan in your smoker to the brim. Soak the charcoal with lighter fluid and let it sit for about ten minutes before lighting. Allow plenty of time for the coals to become covered with ash before you start cooking. While the coals are getting ready, soak a bag of hickory chips

Mix the salt, pepper, dry mustard and garlic powder together. Pour one cup of the apple juice over the Boston butt. Rub the meat with the spice mixture. Pour the rest of the apple juice into your smoker's water pan and fill the rest of the way with water. Drain the hickory chips and place over coals. Place the water pan over the coals and the grill rack over the water pan. Carefully lower the meat onto the grill rack. Cover and leave it alone for 5 hours—tending the fire from time to time, stoking it up and adding coals as needed to keep the temperature up in the medium-high range on your smoker.

After 5 hours, remove the Boston butt from the smoker and wrap it in heavy duty aluminum foil. Place it in an oven heated to 250 for 2 hours. Remove from oven and allow to cool for 30 minutes before pulling it apart. For smaller pieces of meat, use 30 minutes less in the smoker and 30 minutes less in the oven.

Feeds a crowd—about 6-8, depending

Roasted Corn

This is a great side dish that can be cooked right on the grill. It looks great cooking and tastes even better.

6 ears of fresh sweet corn, still in the shucks

butter

salt and pepper

Lawry's Seasoned Salt

Carefully pull back the corn husks, making sure they stay attached to the corn. Remove the silks. Melt the butter slowly and add the salt, pepper and Lawry's. Pull the shucks back up over the corn and secure with toothpicks.

Place the corn on a hot grill. Cook 10-15 minutes, turning frequently. An easier method is to just remove the shucks and wrap the seasoned corn in aluminum foil—but it's not as much fun.

Serves 6.

Beer Can Chicken

Since I now attend a Baptist church the hardest part of making this dish is buying beer without being spotted by members of our congregation. I should be used to it by now because I have been buying it for my mother-in-law for years. She says she needs it to kill snails. But once you have secured a couple of cans of brew—the rest is a snap. The chicken is juicy and tender and delicious and cooking it is fun.

1 4 lb chicken (a fryer)

2 tbsp olive oil

1 tbsp kosher salt

1 tsp black pepper

1 tsp paprika

1 can of beer , half full

Open the beer and discard half the can. What you do with it is your business. Heat the grill. You will use indirect heat, which means you will heat one side of the grill and cook over the other side. Take the giblets and other packaging out of the chicken. Wash the chicken and pat it dry with paper towels, then rub it down with the oil. Mix the other dry ingredients in a small dish and rub the mixture over the oiled chicken.

Set the chicken down over the half-full beer can and set it up on the cool side of the grill, making a tripod out of the beer can and the chicken's two legs. Close the grill and forget about it for an hour. (This is the second hardest part.) After an hour, open the grill and turn the chicken 180 degrees. If you are cooking with charcoal you will probably want to add a few briquettes at this point. Close the grill and cook another 20-30 minutes, until the internal temperature of the thickest part of the bird reaches 160 degrees when tested with a meat thermometer.

Serves 4. Two chickens will serve 8, plus you'll have more beer.

Bourbon Marinated Steak Kabobs

Kentucky folks will take exception with this recipe because I usually use Jack Daniel's Tennessee sipping whiskey, which anybody from the Bluegrass State will tell you is not Bourbon—but the taste is pretty close. If you want to substitute Maker's Mark or Evan Williams—feel free. And if you are a Baptist and thought buying the beer for the chicken was tough—well, just get one of your Methodist friends to pick up the booze for you. Besides—the alcohol all evaporates. That's why you'll want to have a couple of high balls while you are cooking.

2 lbs of sirloin steak

½ cup soy sauce

½ cup Bourbon (or Jack Daniel's)

1/3 cup brown sugar

3 tbsp olive oil

1 tbsp minced garlic

1 tbsp Worcestershire sauce

1 tsp black pepper

1 tsp salt

8 wooden skewers

Cut the steaks up into one inch cubes. Combine the soy sauce, Bourbon, brown sugar, olive oil, garlic, Worcestershire sauce, pepper and salt. Mix well. Place the steak cubes in the marinade and refrigerate overnight. When it is time to cook the steak, soak the skewers in water for 30 minutes. Heat the grill—or allow the coals to get covered with ash—and thread the pieces of steak onto the skewers. Place the skewers on the hot grill and cook for five minutes on each side.

Feeds 3-4 people, depending on appetites

The World's Best Secret Recipe Barbecued Chicken

This is the best thing that Darrell Huckaby cooks—period. And when he is on his A-game, this is as good as anything anybody cooks. But be forewarned—it ain't easy. It takes a good deal of preparation and 90 minutes of constant care. But when you watch the people you serve lick their fingers and stare longingly at the bones—wishing there were more chicken—it will be worth every minute.

2 whole chickens, quartered

Basting Sauce

3 cups water

½ cup lemon juice

½ cup apple cider vinegar

1 tsp salt

1 tbsp black pepper

Barbecue Sauce

¾ cups ketchup

3 tbsp butter

1 medium onion, finely chopped

½ tsp minced garlic

2 tbsp brown sugar

1/3 cup vinegar

1 tsp celery seed

1 tbsp dry mustard

½ tsp salt

2 tsp black pepper

1 tsp red pepper

2 tbsp Worcestershire sauce

1 tsp Tabasco sauce

2 tbsp lemon juice

¼ cup Coca-Cola

Quarter the whole chickens and remove the skin. Wash the chicken pieces and pat dry. Sprinkle with salt and pepper. Meanwhile, of course, the grill is getting ready. (If you are using charcoal, do not use Match-light for this dish. It will not hold the heat long enough. Even with regular charcoal you may need to add charcoal after about 45 minutes.)

Once the grill is ready, place the pieces on the grate, fatty side up. Immediately begin brushing on the basting sauce. For the next 50-60 minutes you will cook the chicken pieces, constantly turning and constantly basting, so the chicken will not cook too fast. (It could take a bit longer, depending on how hot the fire is and the size of the chicken pieces.) The basting sauce keeps it from drying out. When the chicken is almost done, switch to the barbecue sauce, still basting and turning, for another ten minutes or so. If this isn't the best barbecued chicken you ever put in your mouth, you did something wrong.

Grilled Salmon

This dish is quick, easy and healthy—not to mention delicious!

4 salmon filets

6 tbsp butter

2 tbsp lemon juice

salt and pepper

Make sure that the grate on your grill is clean and oiled. Heat your grill to medium. I love to cook some things over charcoal, but the convenience of a good gas grill can't be beat for these kinds of entrees. Melt the butter in a saucepan, being careful not to burn or scorch. Add the lemon juice to the butter. (For a slightly more tart taste you might want to substitute lime juice.) Sprinkle salt and pepper rather liberally over each side of the salmon filets. Place them on the heated grill and brush with half of the lemon-butter mixture. Cook 3-4 minutes, depending on the thickness of the filets. Turn and brush the other side with the remaining lemon-butter and cook 3-4 minutes until flaky. This dish goes great with vegetable rice and a tossed salad. Who said good food has to be fattening?

Makes 4 servings.

Said the old codger to the sweet young thing in the low-cut dress, "I like your outfit."

Said she, "Sho' nuff?"

Said he, "Pret' near."

Southern Fried Catfish Filets

OK, y'all. We fixin' to get serious now. We are about to talk about having a fish fry. I have hosted fish fries on Labor Day, Christmas, St. Patrick's Day, Mother's Day, Memorial Day and just about any and every day in between. Take it from me—there ain't no bad day to have a fish fry. And now that fresh fish is available in grocery stores all over the South, there ain't no excuse to wait for summer. The recipe I'm about to share is for catfish filets, but we cook flounder and even tilapia the same way. It's all good! It really is.

1 gallon cooking oil

2 lbs catfish filets

1 ½ cups corn meal mix

1 tbsp salt

1 tsp black pepper

more salt and pepper

1 egg

1½ cup milk

If the filets are large, split them and cut into 6 inch strips. Large filets take too long to cook and can be either hard on the outside or mushy on the inside. Pour the egg into a medium size bowl and break the egg into the milk. Beat with a whisk for a couple of minutes until thoroughly blended. In an outdoor fish cooker heat the oil to a temperature of 350. Don't heat it too fast or the temperature will keep climbing and cause the fish to cook too fast. Cooking is like making love. Patience is a real virtue. Or so I've been told.

Soak the fish in the milk for about five minutes. Mix the cornmeal mix with the salt and pepper. Remove the fish from the milk mixture and sprinkle with salt and pepper. Roll the fish in the cornmeal—I like to put the cornmeal in a paper sack and just dump the fish in and shake it all around. Place the fish on a piece of wax paper for about five minutes so the breading won't fall off as soon as you drop the fish in the grease.

Drop the fish in the grease and let them cook for about 5-7 minutes, depending on how thick they are. When fish are golden brown, pull them up out of the grease and drain on paper towels. You should cook the fish in small batches and then keep them warm until the whole mess is done.

Serves 5-6

Gladys Rogers's Hell-in-the-Bowl

My mama worked in the mill with a lady named Gladys Rogers and Gladys loved to have fish fries. She introduced me to the delightful dish she called Hell-in-the-Bowl at one of her fish fries and I don't guess I have ever cooked fish without making this dish since then— and I was eight at the time.

2 red ripe tomatoes

1 Vidalia onion

1 green bell pepper

1 red green pepper

2 hot peppers

1 tsp Tabasco sauce

1 cup apple cider vinegar

salt and pepper

Peel and dice the tomatoes. Honesty compels me to admit that I do not peel the tomatoes. You can if you want to. It is really just added time and added mess, if you ask me. Peel and finely chop the onion. You understand, of course, that Vidalias are only available certain times of the year and that you might have to substitute an inferior onion. Finely chop the peppers. Take care with the hot peppers because they can put hair on your chest. The seeds of the hot peppers are, of course, what gives this dish its name. You might want to remove the seeds if you have wimpy guests—or just leave the hot peppers out altogether. Mix the tomatoes, peppers and onions in a serving bowl. Pour enough vinegar over to cover. Sprinkle with salt and black pepper and then add the Tabasco. Makes a great side for fish. Trust me on this one!

There is a funny story about this dish. In 1986 I took an All-Star basketball team to Hawaii to compete. We were being hosted at a luau by a Hawaiian family who served, to my delight, what I thought was Hell-in-the-Bowl. I took a heaping helping. Only when I started trying to eat it did I notice the little bits of pink flesh. They make theirs with raw fish! We used to call that "bait" in Porterdale.

Hushpuppies

I am not sure if it is in the Bible that you have to have these delightful delicacies with fried fish, but if you read Matthew in the original language, I bet you'd find that the word for "loaves" could be translated as "hushpuppies." We always cook the hushpuppies last, in the fish grease, and you will need to let it cool down just a tad to keep them from cooking too fast.

> 2 **eggs**
>
> 2 **cups self-rising cornmeal mix**
>
> 1 **medium onion, finely chopped**
>
> 1 **cup buttermilk**
>
> **pinch of salt**

Mix together the eggs, cornmeal, salt and onion. Slowly add the buttermilk, stirring to blend well. Allow to stand for 2-3 minutes. Using two spoons, drop a teaspoon of batter at a time into the hot oil. Do not crowd as the hushpuppies will need room to float. When they are done on the bottom they will try to roll over. They may flip on their own or you may have to help them along by flipping them with a spoon. When done on both sides remove them with a slotted spoon and drain on paper towels.

Feeds about 6

Benson Plunkett's Beer Batter Fried Shrimp

Benson Plunkett is one of my favorite human beings to ever walk the face of the Earth. He was the first principal at Heritage High School. He is also one of the best outdoor cooks I have ever known—especially seafood. Benson told me that from 1976 until 1980 he had a fish fry every Friday night. He would invite about 20 people—and he said they all came. I don't wonder at it. He would cook 100 catfish and a whole bunch of fried shrimp. This is how he fried his shrimp. Benson says he got the recipe from band director extraordinaire, Carlisle Dent. I guarantee you, it is perfection personified.

> 2 ½ lbs shrimp
>
> ½ cup self rising flour
>
> ½ cup cornstarch
>
> salt and pepper
>
> 2 egg yolks
>
> ½ cup beer
>
> 2 tbsp melted butter
>
> cooking oil

Use large shrimp. Peel the shrimp, leaving the tails intact. Butterfly the shrimp. Mix the flour, cornstarch and salt and pepper together. Separate the yolks from 2 eggs and add to the mixture. Pour ½ cup of milk and melted butter into the batter and mix with a whisk until it is smooth and soupy looking.

Meanwhile, the oil should be heating to 350 degrees. Use a thermometer. Don't guess. When the oil is ready take the shrimp, individually, by the tail and drop into the hot oil. Don't crowd the shrimp. You might need to stir gently with a slotted spoon to keep them from sticking together. The shrimp will be done in 2 ½ to 3 minutes. Remove with a slotted spoon and drain on paper towel and cook the next batch.

Boiled Shrimp

Don't use farm raised shrimp from Vietnam or Thailand. Use wild caught shrimp from the USA. So you spend a couple of extra bucks. The Southern shrimping industry deserves to survive.

2 lbs large shrimp, shell on

water to cover

2 bay leaves

2 tbsp vinegar

2 tbsp lemon juice

1 tsp sugar

1 tsp red pepper

½ cupped handful sea salt

8 peppercorns

Fill a big pot 2/3 to the top with fresh water. Add everything but the shrimp and bring to a boil. Lower the heat and let the water simmer for about 20 minutes. Return to a rolling boil and add the shrimp. Cover and boil for 3 minutes. Pour shrimp into a colander and immediately pour ice water over the shrimp to make them stop cooking. Serve with lemon wedges and cocktail sauce.

Now this is stuff is all good and if you serve up fried and boiled shrimp, fried fish, slaw, Hell-in-the-Bowl, hushpuppies and grits—or maybe a few French fries—you might not ever get rid of your guests! And if they do go home, I promise they'll come back every time you mention a fish fry. Just ask Benson Plunkett if you don't believe me.

Apple Juice Glazed Pork Chops

This is one of my favorites. It is easy enough for a Tuesday night supper and good enough for Saturday night company.

4-8 center loin pork chops

1 qt apple juice

½ cup honey

2 tbsp soy sauce

1 tbsp brown sugar

1 tbsp lemon juice

Combine apple juice, honey, soy sauce, sugar and lemon juice. Salt and pepper the pork chops and marinate them in the apple juice mixture for 2-3 hours before time to cook. Place the chops on a medium hot grill and cook until done, 25-35 minutes, depending on the thickness. Turn often and baste with the reserve marinade each time you turn the meat. (Some people advise bringing the marinade to a boil in a microwave before basting the cooking chops and some people even make a separate batch of marinade.)

Feeds 4

Apricot Glazed Pork Loin

1 2 lb. pork loin

1 jar apricot preserves

salt and pepper

Split the pork loin in half lengthwise and sprinkle liberally with salt and pepper. Pour the apricot preserves over the loin, spreading evenly with a butter knife. Refrigerate for two hours. Place the loin on a medium-hot grill and cook 10-12 minutes on each side, basting with the preserves as you cook. Slice and serve.

Feeds 4

Fairly Easy Baby Back Ribs

I have tried lots and lots of ways of cooking ribs. I have smoked them and par-boiled them before grilling them and done all sorts of things people tell you do—as well as lots of things people tell you not to do. If you are trying to win a rib cook-off in Memphis, this recipe isn't nearly complicated enough. If you want to cook something really good for your family or friends—give it a try. You'll like it!

> **2 racks of baby back ribs**
>
> **4 tbsp Liquid Smoke**
>
> **1 tbsp salt**
>
> **2 tbsp black pepper**
>
> **1 tsp red pepper**
>
> **1 tsp paprika**
>
> **2 tsp dry mustard**
>
> **½ tsp garlic powder**
>
> **½ tsp onion powder**

Barbecue Sauce from above recipe

Cut each rack of ribs into 2 pieces. Rub the ribs with the liquid smoke. Combine the next 7 dry ingredients. Rub the ribs with the dry rub and wrap each piece separately in aluminum foil. Place a tbsp of water on each piece of ribs before wrapping. Bake at 250 for 2 ½ hours. Remove from oven and cook another 20 to 30 minutes over a medium hot grill, basting with barbecue sauce and turning frequently the last 10-15 minutes.

Serves 4

Sirloin Kabobs

Jeff "Stump" Autry taught me to make these. He and I even went in together and bought a set of metal skewers one time. Jeff has been gone way too long. I'm not sure what happened to those skewers, but I know that I think about Jeff every time I make this recipe—and I smile.

2 lbs sirloin steak

½ cup soy sauce

1 tbsp olive oil

3 tbsp brown sugar

½ tsp garlic powder

½ tsp salt

½ tsp black pepper

1 tbsp lemon juice

½ tsp ground ginger

1 fresh pineapple

2 medium onions

½ lb fresh mushroom

1 green bell pepper

1 red bell pepper

2 cups cherry tomatoes

12—16 wooden skewers

Cut the steak into 1 inch cubes. Combine the next eight ingredients to make the marinade. Marinate the steak overnight. Peel and core the pineapple (or buy a fresh pineapple that is peeled and cored.)

Here is a trick I learned while visiting Hawaii. For a sweeter pineapple, cut off the top and turn the pineapple upside down onto a plate for an hour or two before using. The sugar will run down and make the fruit sweeter.

Soak the skewers in water for about 30 minutes. Cut the pineapple into one inch chunks and the onions and peppers into 1 inch squares.

Remove the meat from the marinade, saving the marinade for basting. Thread the skewers, alternating the steak, pineapple, peppers, onions, mushrooms and tomatoes. Grill over medium hot coals for 10-12 minutes, turning frequently and basting with marinade.

Makes 4-6 servings.

Holiday Smoked Turkey

We have never cooked "the turkey" at our house on Thanksgiving. We have always celebrated somewhere else. But I love leftover turkey sandwiches, which is a problem when there is no leftover turkey. I figured out how to solve that problem a few years ago. Now I smoke a turkey every year on the Monday before Thanksgiving, while I am smoking the Boston butt for the Brunswick stew. Problem solved. We have plenty of delicious, flavorful turkey for the entire holiday weekend.

1 12-14 pound fresh turkey

1 apples

2 stalks of celery

8 whole pecans

1 medium onion

2 tbsp olive oil

salt and pepper

Prepare the smoker by filling the charcoal pan to the top, soaking the coals with lighter fluid and letting the coals sit for about ten minutes. Then light the fire and while the coals are getting ready, soak a big handful of hickory chunks—or mesquite if you prefer—in water until the coals are covered with white ash.

Use a fresh turkey. You don't want it to be too big because it takes too long to get done. A 12-14 pound bird is a great size. If you are trying to feed a big crowd, you can smoke two almost as easily as one. Remove the giblets and wash the turkey, inside and out. Pat it dry with a paper towel and then rub it down well with the olive oil and sprinkle it liberally with salt and pepper. Peel and quarter the onion. Core the apples and cut into quarters. Wash the celery and cut each stalk into about four pieces and stuff all of the fruit and vegetables, as well as the pecans, inside the turkey. Use wooden skewers to close up the opening so they won't fall out.

Once the coals are ready, place the hickory chips on top of the coals and set a full water pan on top of the fire. Place the turkey on the grill, just over the water pan. Cover and allow it to smoke for about 30 minutes per pound before taking the top off the smoker to check it. You'll want to, but resist the temptation. Trust me! You'll be a better person for it. Also keep in mind that the temperature of the fire and the outside temperature will greatly affect cooking time. The 30 minutes per pound is simply a rule of thumb.

You will want to stoke up your fire and add charcoal about every hour— and maybe more hickory chunks the first couple of times. Try to keep the smoker toward around 250, if it has a temperature gauge. The only way to know if the bird is done is to check it with a meat thermometer. 165 at the thickest part is the magic number.

Have fun and enjoy the leftovers—if there are any.

Wine Marinated London Broil

The London Broil is a less expensive cut of meat, which makes it a good choice if you are feeding a crowd or if you just want a mouthful of something tasty without getting choked on the cost. It can be a might tough if you don't cook it right. This is one way to cook it right.

> ¼ **cup dry red wine**
>
> 2 **tbsp soy sauce**
>
> 2 **tbsp balsamic vinegar**
>
> 1 **tbsp Dijon mustard**
>
> ¼ **tsp crushed red peppers**
>
> 1 **tsp minced garlic**
>
> 1 **London broil (2 lbs)**

Mix the first 6 ingredients in small bowl until well blended and pour into a gallon freezer bag. Add the steak and make sure it gets well coated. Refrigerate for at least 5 or 6 hours—overnight is even better. You will want to turn the steak every once in a while.

Prepare your grill and cook the steak for about 15 minutes (for medium), or until it reaches your desired doneness. Remove the steak from the grill and let it sit for about 10 minutes. Then slice the steak with a sharp knife, making thin slices across the grain.

Makes 6 servings

Hay Hauling Hamburgers

We have a longstanding custom on my father-in-law's farm that, after the hay is in the barn, we all get together for a cookout around the pool—and hamburgers are better around the pool after a hot afternoon in the hayfield than they are just about anywhere else. But they are still great, no matter the circumstances.

2 lbs ground chuck

Worcestershire sauce

salt and pepper

garlic salt

buns

sliced Vidalia onions

sliced tomatoes

mustard

ketchup

dill chips

Form the ground beef into 8 patties by rolling them into balls and flattening them out between your palms. Sprinkle each side with salt, pepper, a touch of garlic salt and a dab of Worcestershire sauce. Cook on a medium hot grill, about six or seven minutes on a side. Turn when the clear juices begin to run through. For great cheeseburgers add thick slices of your favorite cheese to the top of the burgers during the last couple of minutes. I prefer to warm the buns in the oven because I invariably burn my hands on them when I warm them on the grill—plus, a grill hot enough to cook burgers is too hot to warm the buns without charring them.

Serve with all of the above fixings, an assortment of chips and maybe some of my doctored up baked beans. And don't forget the fruit salad. And if you really want to find out how good a hamburger can taste, come help us out in the hayfield one day and find out for yourself.

2 large can Bush's Best Baked Beans

4 slices bacon, cut in half

½ cup ketchup

2 tbsp prepared mustard

½ cup brown sugar

Mix the beans, ketchup and mustard and brown sugar. Pour into a 9x11 baking dish and lay the strips of bacon on top. Bake at 350 for about 40-45 minutes.

Easy Dutch Oven Peach Cobbler

Got to have at least one dessert option for a cookout. This is one that our friend Clay Stapp makes on our annual Jekyll Island Spring Break campouts—right before we go out and hunt wild boar by moonlight.

2 cans (30 oz) sliced peaches, drained

1 can Sprite

1 yellow cake mix, dry

4 tbsp butter

1 tbsp cinnamon

Spread the canned peaches out on the bottom of an outdoor Dutch oven. Pour the cake mix over the peaches and then pour the Sprite over both, stirring to mix completely. Place a few tabs of butter over the top and sprinkle the cinnamon over everything. Place the Dutch oven over a dozen hot charcoal briquettes and place a dozen more hot briquettes on top. Match Light charcoal doesn't work well as it burns out too rapidly. Cook for 45 minutes, rotating the oven and the lid every 15 minutes. Peek in after 45 minutes. If not quite done, return lid and cook for another 15 minutes.

Annual Jekyll Island Seafood Boil

Bob Bradley's Big Green Egg Smoked Turkey

My buddy Bob Bradley, who is also one of my many bosses, makes the big bucks and owns a Big Green Egg. If you will tell everybody you know to order a copy of this book, maybe I can afford one someday. He swears by his and I have tasted some of the victuals he has prepared. They are pretty dang good. He was kind enough to share a couple of them.

½ cup salt

½ cup cracked pepper

¼ cup black pepper

2 tbsp white vinegar

Dijon mustard

Grind all dry ingredients. Add vinegar to mixture to make paste. Cover turkey breast with mustard then put paste on turkey. This will make a crust on your turkey. Smoke on Green Egg at 300 degrees until turkey reaches 165 degrees internally. If you don't have a Big Green Egg, use a regular smoker grill. It will take longer.

Smoked Jalapeno Peppers

10-12 jalapenos

1 lb ground beef

1 pkg taco seasoning

16 oz cream cheese softened

1 lb uncooked bacon

Cut jalapenos long ways and clean out seeds. Brown ground beef and drain fat. Add taco seasoning and cream cheese to beef. Cook till well mixed. Stuff peppers with mixture and wrap with bacon. Smoke on green egg until bacon is crispy. This can be done on a regular grill as well.

Hal Bush's South Georgia Style Grilled Venison Loin

Hal Bush is one of the best people I know. Hal is from way below the gnat line—in Albany, Georgia. He and I taught together at Heritage High School and I guarantee you, the two of us sat and solved all the problems of the world during last period planning. And if Mark Richt had been a fly on our wall, Georgia would have been undefeated from 2001 until forever. We had all the answers. Hal bailed on me. He retired. But I am going to join him soon—as soon as I sell enough of these books to buy that Big Green Egg from the previous recipes. Hal is a hunter—and this is one of the ways he likes to cook his deer.

1 ½ lbs venison, cubed

1 cup Italian salad dressing

½ cup soy sauce

1 tbsp minced garlic

1 lb bacon, thin sliced

Combine the Italian dressing, soy sauce and garlic to make the marinade. Place the venison in a pan and pour the marinade over the meat. Cover and place in a refrigerator for about an hour. When ready to cook, remove from the marinade and wrap the venison cubes with the bacon strips. (Secure with a toothpick.) Cook on medium hot grill for about 3-4 minutes on each side. Do not overcook!

Glad Somebody Went Hunting Deer Roast

1 3-4 lb venison roast

1 ½ tsp onion powder, divided

1 tsp garlic powder

1 tsp salt

1 tsp black pepper

7 **carrots, quartered**

4 **small onions, quartered**

1 **tbsp beef bullion granules**

2 **tbsp Worcestershire sauce**

2 **tbsp cornstarch**

3 **tbsp cold water**

Make several cuts in the roast to allow seasonings to be more easily absorbed. Combine 1 tsp of the onion powder, the garlic powder, salt and pepper and rub well over the roast. Cover and refrigerate 2 hours. Put ½ inch of water in the bottom of a roasting pan. Add the roast, the carrots and the onions. Cover and bake at 325 for 2 ½ to 3 hours. Place the roast and vegetables on a serving platter and keep warm. Take the leavings from the roast and combine with enough water to make 3 cups. Add the Worcestershire sauce and rest of the onion powder. Combine the cornstarch with the water and add the pan leavings. Bring to a boil and cook until thickened. Serve with the roast as a gravy.

North Avenue Tailgate Fare

Now everybody that knows me knows that I bleed red and black and when the calendar says that fall is upon us, I am going to be wherever the Georgia Bulldogs happen to be playing. And as with all true Georgia fans, my two favorite teams are the Dawgs and whoever is playing Georgia Tech.

But I do have some friends who are Tech fans. Anthony Norton and Alton McCullough are as true-blue for the Jackets as I am for the Dawgs, and I guarantee you, their tailgates would be top drawer in Athens or The Grove at Ole Miss or anywhere else Southern college football is played. Alton, who bears a striking resemblance to Santa Claus, was kind enough to share a couple of his favorite recipes—so even Wayne Kerr and Melinda Sileo can feel good about owning this book.

Grilled Chicken with White BBQ Sauce

2 cups Blue Plate Mayonnaise

1 cup white wine vinegar

¼ cup lemon juice

2 tbsp ground black pepper

2 tbsp salt

4 tbsp sugar

Mix all ingredients together. Next take your favorite chicken pieces and grill to your personal specs. During the last 10 minutes baste the chicken with the sauce. Turn the chicken and baste both sides. If desired, top cooked chicken with the remaining sauce.

Tailgate Chili

1 lb ground chuck

2 10 oz cans diced tomatoes and green chilies (liquid included)

1 15 oz can red kidney beans (liquid drained)

1 15 oz can pinto beans (liquid drained)

1 8 oz can tomato sauce

1 ½ tbsp dried chopped onions

2 tbsp chili powder

½ tbsp ground cumin

1 tsp salt

½ tsp ground black pepper

¼ tsp garlic powder

1 cup water

Brown the ground chuck over medium heat, breaking into small pieces with a spatula. Drain the grease. Place all other ingredients into a 4 qt crock pot. Stir well. Add the ground chuck and cook over low heat for about 6 hours. Add your favorite toppings—chopped onions, cheese, jalapenos—and enjoy. This can be made the day before the game and heated up.

Hot Dog Sauce

Believe it or not, *The Varsity* has the second best hotdogs on North Avenue when Tech is playing at home. Alton and Anthony and their crowd have the best—primarily because of this killer sauce. It's good enough for a Dawg to enjoy!

- **2 tbsp olive oil**
- **2 tbsp beef broth**
- **2 tbsp dried chopped onions**
- **1 6oz can tomato paste**
- **½ cup water**
- **3 tbsp vinegar**
- **¼ cup sweet pickle relish**
- **1 tsp salt**
- **2 tsp prepared mustard**
- **1 tsp chili powder**
- **¼ tsp ground black pepper**
- **1 dash cayenne pepper**

Soak the onions in broth until reconstituted and then brown the onions in oil. Stir in the tomato paste, water, vinegar, pickle relish, salt, and mustard. Simmer for 25 minutes. Blend in the seasonings and simmer for 5 minutes longer. Serve over grilled hotdogs or brats.

Company's
Coming

Company's Comin'

If you haven't figured it out by now, let me fill you in. We have always eaten pretty well at our house. Food is a big priority. Now you can't tell that by looking at my wife or kids but it is a bit more apparent when you see me. We eat well, but not necessarily high on the hog. Once in a great while, however—maybe on a holiday or some other special occasion—we do put on the dog and invite company over. The recipes in this chapter are what we might fix on those occasions.

I will also go ahead and tell you that we are big on tradition. If we happen to have the same meal twice on any given day, chances are more than even that we will have that dish on that day until the cows come home. Now corned beef and cabbage is a given on St. Patrick's Day, as is pork roast and collards on New Year's. And we will have ham and deviled eggs and potato salad on Easter and a fish fry on Memorial Day and barbecue and watermelon on the 4th of July and shrimp Creole or barbecued shrimp on Fat Tuesday. And we will have hot dogs on Opening Day of the baseball season.

You will notice that a lot of these recipes are well suited for holidays— and that there are few "summer" recipes mentioned. We do a lot of outside cooking in the summer time when company comes. But please don't limit these delicious meals to holiday entertaining. They are good anytime.

But you get my drift. Keep turning pages and see if you find something that you might want to turn into a tradition at your house. If so—remember, the title of the chapter is "Company's Comin'" and if I don't qualify as company, I don't know who does. Give me a call when dinner is ready!

New Year's Day Pork Roast

Everybody knows that you eat some part of a pig's rump on New Year's Day, along with black-eyed peas for luck and collard greens for prosperity. Green is, after all the color of money. And at our house we also eat sweet potatoes simply because they taste so good and cornbread simply because. This is how I cook our pork on New Year's Day.

1 5-6 lb pork loin roast (or Boston Butt)

2 ½ tbsp Liquid Smoke

1 banana

2 ½ tbsp coarse salt

2 tsp black pepper

Rub the pork with the Liquid Smoke, then mash the banana and rub it all over the pork as well. Sprinkle with salt and pepper and wrap tightly in foil. Place in a pan and bake at 350 for about 45 minutes per pound of meat. When done the pork should pull apart easily with your fingers.

If this ain't tasty, a pig's rump ain't pork!

St. Valentine's Day Shrimp Creole

One of the first meals Lisa and I had as husband and wife was shrimp Creole, at the French Market Restaurant, near Jackson Square, in New Orleans. Ever since then shrimp Creole has been one of our favorite dishes when we want to enjoy a romantic evening at home. But it is good any time—and way too good not to share with company.

½ cup onion, chopped

½ cup celery, chopped

½ cup green pepper, chopped

3 tbsp oil

1 16 oz can diced tomatoes

1 8 oz can tomato sauce

1 ½ tsp salt

1 tsp sugar

1 tsp chili powder

1 tbsp Worcestershire sauce

1 tsp Tabasco sauce

2 tsp cornstarch

1 lb raw shrimp, peeled

Sauté the onions, celery and green pepper in oil until tender. Add the tomatoes, tomato sauce, salt, sugar, chili powder, Worcestershire and Tabasco. Simmer uncovered for 30 minutes. Mix the cornstarch with about a tbsp of water and stir into the sauce. Continue to cook, stirring, until the mixture thickens and begins to bubble. Add the shrimp, cover and simmer 5-7 minutes until shrimp is done. Serve over cooked rice with a nice green salad and French bread and Cupid will do the rest. It works every time!

Fat Tuesday Barbecued Shrimp

We love the New Orleans culture. Cajun, Creole . . . you name it, we try to cook it. And New Orleans food just seems to scream "party." You got to have lots of company to enjoy a party. These dishes beg for a crowd. The barbecued shrimp recipe feeds 10. Cut it down if you don't have that many mouths to feed. And for the record, it is not really barbecued at all, but a chef at Pascal's Manale Restaurant in N'awlins named it and who am I to argue with a chef at Pascal's? This version of the dish comes from Lisa's friend, Dale. And before you ask, that's not a misprint on the butter.

2 lbs butter

2 tbsp Creole seasoning

or

3 tsp red cayenne pepper and 3 tsp black pepper

2 tbsp chopped rosemary leaves

½ cup Worcestershire Sauce

6 oz beer

5 cloves garlic, minced

1 medium onion, finely chopped

3 ribs celery, chopped

3 tbsp chopped parsley

2 tsp freshly squeezed lemon juice

5 lbs large shrimp, shells on

Melt one stick of the butter in a large skillet. Sauté the garlic, onions, celery, parsley, rosemary and seasoning over medium heat for about 3-4 minutes. Melt the rest of the butter in a large pan. Add the beer, the sautéed stuff, the Worcestershire sauce and the lemon juice.

Now drown the shrimp in the butter and bake at 350 for about 15 minutes. Serve the dish up in bowls, making sure to spoon out plenty of shrimp and plenty of the butter mixture. Serve with good French bread. Sopping is not only encouraged, it is mandatory. Have plenty of paper towels on hand—and maybe a few bibs. And remember—if it is Fat Tuesday, Lent begins at midnight.

Feeds 10

"You got your shoes on your feet--on Bourbon Street, in New Orleans, LA-- USA! Now pay me my $10!"

St. Paddy's Day Corned Beef and Cabbage

1 **3 lb corned beef brisket with spice package**

10 **small red new potatoes**

5 **carrots, peeled and cut into thirds**

1 **cabbage, cut into small wedges**

Place the corned beef and the spice packet in a large pot and cover with water. Bring to a boil and then lower heat and simmer for about 50 minutes. Add the potatoes and carrots and cook for another 15 minutes. Add the cabbage and cook 15 more minutes. Remove the vegetables to a separate serving dish and ladle some of the broth over them. Slice the corned beef against the grain and serve.

Erin go Bragh, y'all!

Serves 4-5

Easter Baked Ham

I'm sorry. On Easter Sunday I want ham, and as easy as it is to stand in line at the HoneyBaked Ham store and pick up one of theirs, we just prefer to cook our own. And we always have to serve it with potato salad, green beans and Easter eggs—oops, I meant to say deviled eggs. Here's how we do the ham.

1 10-12 pound fresh bone-in ham

½ cup whole cloves

1 cup brown sugar

3 cups water

1 cup pineapple juice

Prepare the ham by placing the cloves in the top at 1 to 2 inch intervals. Be sure to make a pretty criss-cross pattern. Place in a large roasting pan and pour the pineapple juice over the ham. Pat down the top of the ham with a layer of brown sugar. Pour about an inch of water into the bottom of the pan. Cover with heavy foil and bake at 350 for about 4 ½ to 5 hours—about 20 minutes per pound. The ham is done when a meat thermometer inserted into the center reaches 160 degrees. Remove the ham from the oven and let stand before slicing.

Lisa's Perfect Deviled Easter Eggs

But they are good anytime and a must at a tailgate party.

13 eggs (an extra one for the filling)

½ cup mayonnaise

½ tsp salt

1 tbsp yellow mustard

2 tbsp sweet pickles, finely chopped

Paprika

Hard boil the eggs by placing in a large boiler and covering with water, an inch above the eggs. Turn the heat to medium and bring the water to a boil. Turn down and allow the water to simmer for 10 minutes. Turn off the heat and let the eggs set for another 10 minutes. Cool down in cold water and peel.

Cut the eggs in half and reserve yolks to a large bowl. Mash the yolks with a fork and add the mustard, pickles and then gradually add the mayonnaise, constantly stirring, until it is the desired consistency. There is nothing worse, to me, than soupy deviled eggs. Add the salt and stir enough to blend and stuff the 24 egg halves with the mixture. Sprinkle lightly with paprika.

Potato Salad

6 medium potatoes

2 hard boiled eggs

½ to ¾ cups mayonnaise

1 tsp mustard

½ cup sweet salad cubes

1 tsp salt

½ tsp celery seed

Peel the potatoes and cut into small cubes. Boil the potatoes in salted water until a fork pierces them fairly easy. You don't want them mushy. Pour the potatoes into a colander. Rinse and allow to cool. Mix the mayonnaise, mustard, salt, celery seed and pickles together. Gently toss over the potatoes and chopped eggs. If it looks too dry add a little more mayonnaise and then salt to taste. Refrigerate until ready to serve.

Serves 8

Hash Brown Potato Casserole

1 2 lb pkg shredded hash browns, thawed

½ cup butter, melted

1 cup cream of chicken soup

2 cups cheddar cheese, grated

1 tsp salt

¼ tsp pepper

16 oz sour cream

½ cup finely chopped onion

Topping

2 cups cornflakes

½ stick butter

Mix all ingredients in a large bowl. Pour into a buttered 13x9 casserole dish. Make the topping by crushing the cornflakes and combining the cornflakes and the melted butter. Sprinkle the topping evenly over the top and bake the potato dish at 350 for 45 minutes.

Serves 8

Memo to all Northern immigrants: We really don't care how good y'all think you can drive on ice and snow!"

Elegant Shrimp and Grits

There are as many ways to make shrimp and grits these days as there are folks who try to cook shrimp and grits. This is my recipe.

2 cups water

1 cups chicken broth

1 cup milk

salt and pepper

1 cup course ground grits (Nora Mills, if available)

4 tbsp butter

1 1/2 cups shredded cheddar cheese

1 pound shrimp, peeled

6 slices cooked bacon, chopped

1/4 cup thinly sliced green onions

1 tsp minced garlic

In a pretty good sized pot, combine the water, chicken broth and a little salt and bring to a boil. Add grits and cook until the water is absorbed. This should take between 20 and 25 minutes. Remove from heat and stir in the butter, cheese and black pepper to taste.

Fry the bacon in a large skillet. Remove from pan and drain well on paper towel. When bacon is cool, crumble it up. Add the shrimp to the bacon grease and cook until they turn pink—about 3 minutes. Add the lemon juice, crumbled bacon, onions and garlic and sauté for about 3 more minutes.

Spoon the grits into a serving bowl and top with the shrimp and pan leavings. Stir well to combine the flavors.

Makes 4 servings

Chicken Divan

This is Dolores Evans's recipe. It serves four, but since these dishes are for company, go ahead and plan on doubling it. That's what she does automatically.

2 10 oz pkgs frozen broccoli

3 cups chopped cooked chicken breasts

2 cans cream of chicken soup

1 cup mayonnaise

1 cup shredded cheddar cheese

Cook the broccoli according to the package directions and drain. Arrange in the bottom of a greased baking dish. Place the chicken over the broccoli. Mix the soup and mayonnaise and pour over the chicken. Bake uncovered for 30 minutes at 350. Top with cheese and bake another 10 minutes.

Becky Cavan's Company Cheese Grits

You might wonder why this recipe wasn't in the breakfast chapter. It is just too danged good to have when it's just your family at home. Becky Cavan sent me this recipe. Her husband, Mike, was a pretty fair country football player at the University of Georgia back in the 1960s and a pretty fair country football coach after that. Becky's father-in-law, Jim Cavan, was one of the best high school coaches the state of Georgia has ever known. And Becky—well, obviously, in addition to being a beautiful lady, she cooks a heck of a pot of grits!

Grits

1 quart whole milk

1 cup hominy grits

½ cup butter (cut in pieces)

1 tsp salt

1/8 tsp pepper

Topping

1/3 cup butter, melted

1 cup grated Gruyere cheese

1/3 cup Parmesan cheese

In a large pot, bring the milk to a boil. Add the butter (cut up in pieces). Gradually stir in the grits. Bring the mixture to a boil, mixing until the consistency of Cream of Wheat. Add salt and pepper. Beat with an electric mixer until creamy. Pour mixture in buttered casserole (oblong Pyrex) and let stand until hard. Cut congealed grits into rectangles (about 1 x 1 ½ inches each). Place rectangles in a shallow oven proof (buttered) serving dish, domino style. Pour melted butter over top of grits. Sprinkle grated cheeses over top.

Bake uncovered in a 400 degree oven for 30-35 minutes until a light golden brown. Note!! Watch to make sure it does not burn!

This makes 6 servings. If you want 12 servings, simply double the recipe. Your company will thank you!

Sunday Dinner Company Roast Chicken

4 to 5 lb. young roaster chicken

1 tbsp salt

Remove the giblets from inside the chicken and wash and pat dry. Sprinkle the salt on the outside of the chicken. Wrap tightly in foil and bake at 350 for about 2 hours. Open the foil the last 30 minutes. Drain the juices and retain for the gravy.

Southern Cornbread Dressing

4 cups cornbread crumbs

5 biscuits, crumbled

3 cups hot broth

2 raw eggs, slightly beaten

3 tablespoon minced onion

1 cup finely chopped celery

1 tsp sage

½ tsp black pepper

First you have to cook a pan of cornbread and a pan of biscuits. You might want to do this a day ahead. Place the bread crumbs in a large mixing bowl. Heat the chicken broth to boiling and add the hot broth to the bread crumbs and let it set for about 5 minutes. Add other ingredients in the order listed. Use more broth if the mixture appears too dry. Pour into a well greased 9x13 baking dish. Bake at 350 for about an hour, until golden brown. Serve with giblet gravy and cranberry sauce.

Giblet Gravy

2 cups chicken broth

flour

½ tsp salt

1 chopped hard boiled egg

cooked gizzard and or liver/optional

Pour 2 cups of broth into a small sauce pan. Whisk in enough flour to make the gravy thicken. Add the salt, the chopped egg and the chopped giblets (if you are using them). Cook until thickened, stirring constantly. Some people have been known to reserve a tsp of the uncooked dressing to add to the gravy to give it a little more body, as well as great tatse.

Thanksgiving-Worthy Cranberry Sauce

1 pkg Ocean Spray fresh cranberries

1 cup water

½ cup orange juice

1 cup sugar

Combine all ingredients and bring to a boil. Continue to boil until the berries begin to pop. (You'll know.) Boil for about ten more minutes, until the mixture thickens. Pour into a bowl and refrigerate.

Aunt Sarah's Annual Thanksgiving Feast

Broccoli and Rice Casserole

This dish, as well as the hash brown casserole, is great with my barbecued chicken. Serve that meal to your friends and they will never want
to eat at home again.

¼ cup finely chopped onion

1/3 cup chopped celery

3 tbsp butter, melted

2 10 oz pkg frozen broccoli

2 cups cooked Minute Rice

1 can cream of chicken soup

2/3 cup milk

8 oz Velveeta cheese

salt and pepper

Cook the rice and broccoli according to the directions on the package.
Sauté the onion and celery in butter until tender. Add the cooked broccoli and all other ingredients except the rice. Simmer for about 5-10
minutes, until well blended. Add the cooked rice and bake, uncovered,
at 350 for 30 minutes.

Serves 8

Sweet Potato Soufflé

3 cups mashed sweet potatoes

1 cup sugar

2 eggs

1 ½ tsp salt

1/3 stick butter

½ cup milk

1 tsp vanilla

Topping

1 ½ cups brown sugar

½ cup flour

1 cup chopped pecans

½ stick butter

Boil the sweet potatoes until they are very tender. If you can stick a fork in them, they are done. Drain the water. Peel the potatoes and mash them in a large bowl. Add all the remaining ingredients and mix well. Pour the mixture into a greased casserole dish.

To make the topping, melt the butter and stir in the flour and brown sugar. The mixture should be crumbly. Stir in the nuts and distribute evenly over the potatoes. Bake at 350 for 40-45 minutes.

Makes 8 servings

Christmas Time Standing Rib Roast

We have this once or twice during the Christmas season. It gives us a chance to bring out the good china and the silver and make use of all the wedding gifts we received back in 1982. And then we don't have it again until the next Christmas—or use the good china. Go figure.

Prime rib roast

2 tbsp butter

2 tsp kosher salt

2 tsp coarse black pepper

Allow the roast to warm to room temperature. Preheat oven to 450. Rub the outside of the roast with butter and sprinkle with salt and pepper. Place the roast, fat side up, in a heavy roasting pan. Sear the roast at 450 for 15 minutes, then lower the temperature to 325. Do not cover the roast. Every 30 minutes, baste the top and sides with the liquid that is accumulating in the bottom of the pan.

Cooking times will obviously vary, but count on 2-2 ½ hours. Start checking with a meat thermometer about 45 minutes before you anticipate the roast will be done. The internal temperature inserted into the thickest part of the roast will read 125 for medium rare. Keep in mind that the roast will continue to cook after you remove it from the oven.

When done to your liking, remove from heat and let stand for 20 minutes before carving. Serve with roasted new red potatoes, asparagus, elegant green salad and rolls for a meal to remember.

Horseradish Sauce

½ cup prepared horseradish

1 pint sour cream

2 tbsp freshly squeezed lemon juice

1 tsp salt

In a medium sized bowl combine all ingredients and mix well. Refrigerate before serving.

Roasted New Potatoes

12-14 new red potatoes (small)

1 pkg Lipton Onion Soup mix

½ cup sour cream

6 tbsp butter

½ cup grated cheddar cheese

salt and pepper

Scrub the potatoes well and arrange them in a well greased 9x13 baking dish. Soften the butter and combine with the sour cream and soup mix. Pour evenly over the potatoes and sprinkle with salt and pepper. Cover with foil and bake at 350 for about 40 minutes, or until golden brown. During the last ten minutes, remove the foil and sprinkle the cheese over the potatoes and complete cooking uncovered.

Makes 6 servings

Asparagus Divine

4 tbsp butter

1 tbsp minced garlic

2 bunches fresh asparagus

½ cup red wine

Trim the asparagus and cut into 2 inch pieces. Melt the butter in a large skillet over medium heat. Sauté the garlic for about three minutes. Add the asparagus and cook, covered, for about 2 minutes. Add the wine and cook uncovered until the wine has evaporated and the asparagus is tender. About 4-5 minutes.

Soups, Salads, Snacks, and Such...

Soups, Salads, Snacks and Such

Sometimes a person just wants a bowl of soup. Sometimes they want a salad. Sometimes they want a soup and a salad and sometimes they want something else entirely. Whether you like to have soup or salad as a meal or with a meal or instead of a meal, these are some of our favorites and I would bet a gold tooth that you will find something in here that you'll find fittin' to eat.

But the chapter is entitled Soups, Salads, Snacks and Such. The snacks are the special little treats that make life more fun—appetizers, some people call them. Whether you need something to put on the table at an autumn tailgate, or whether it is your turn to host the Super Bowl get-together, we're sure you will find something in here to delight everyone gathered around your table.

Plus, we've thrown in a couple of things just because we wanted you to know about them and didn't know where else to put them.

Soup's on, y'all! Eat up!

First the Soups!

Tommie Huckaby's Brunswick Stew

This is my mama's recipe for Brunswick stew and takes about two days to make. It is messy and a lot of work—and it's well worth it. I usually make it once a year—the week of Thanksgiving. We eat a lot of it and I give a lot of it away, to people I am especially thankful for. And we freeze a lot of it for later. Give it a try. My mama would be tickled.

2 lb each, cooked beef, pork, chicken

   broth from chicken and pork

4 medium potatoes

3 medium onions

2 large cans tomatoes

   juice of ½ lemon

2 tsp red pepper

1 tbsp dry mustard

1 tbsp brown sugar

¼ cup Worcestershire sauce

1 large can whole kernel corn

½ lb butter

   salt and pepper

I make this a two day process. The first day I smoke the pork, boil and debone the chicken and roast the beef. The second day I grind the meat and vegetables and cook the stew. If you want to feed a huge crowd, triple the recipe and cook it in a big black pot outside. You can stir it with a clean canoe paddle.

Cook the meat, then debone and grind it. I use a KitchenAid food processor with the coarse grinding attachment. Grind the potatoes and onions and cook over medium heat in the broth and tomatoes. You have to stir often or the vegetables will stick to the bottom of the pot and burn. Add the meat and the next 5 ingredients. Cook for 30-45 more minutes. Add the corn and butter and simmer for 30 more minutes, stirring often. Add salt and pepper to taste.

Oyster Stew

We have this dish often, during the winter—but always, always, always on whatever day it is that we decorate our Christmas tree.

½ cup butter

½ cup minced celery

½ cup minced onion

1 cup half-and-half

3 cups milk

1 pint fresh oysters

salt and pepper

Melt the butter in a heavy boiler and sauté the celery and onions. Add the oysters and simmer over low heat for about 5 minutes, until oysters begin to curl just a bit at the edges. Add the milk and half-and-half as well as the salt and pepper. Slowly heat until the milk is well blended and warm throughout. Do not allow to boil.

Makes 4-6 servings

Chicken Stew

I once wrote a newspaper column lamenting the fact that I did not have my mama's recipe for chicken stew. I was deluged with suggestions from my readers—and introduced to something I had never had called chicken mull. After a lot of experimenting and a lot of combining recipes I finally came up with this simple recipe that is about as close to my mama's as I could hope to get.

1 lb cooked chicken, shredded

1 cup chicken broth

1 8 oz can stewed tomatoes

2 cups milk

2 tbsp butter

salt and pepper

In a medium boiler, combine all ingredients but milk. Cook about 30 minutes then add milk, keep almost to a boil, watching carefully so as not to allow the milk to curdle. Reduce heat and simmer 20 minutes. Serve with plenty of soda crackers. (If you are younger than 55 or did not have the great fortune to have been raised in the South, those are saltines.)

Makes 5-6 servings

Lisa's Bless Her Heart Southern Seafood Gumbo

We aren't Cajuns, but wish we could be—at least when we find ourselves in the mood for some delicious Cajun food—which is often. They say it is all the roux—and Lisa has about done got gumbo figured out. There's a lot of stuff and it's a lot of work—and it is sooo worth it!

½ cup vegetable oil

½ cup all purpose flour

4 ribs celery, chopped

2 medium onions, chopped

1 small green pepper, chopped

1 clove minced garlic

½ lb okra, sliced

1 tbsp vegetable oil

1 qt chicken broth (homemade stock even better)

4 cups water

½ cup Worcestershire sauce

2 tsp Tabasco sauce

¼ cup ketchup

1 small tomato, chopped

1 tsp salt

2 slices bacon, chopped

1 bay leaf

½ tsp dried thyme

½ tsp dried rosemary

¼ tsp red pepper

2 lbs unpeeled fresh wild caught shrimp

2 cups chopped cooked chicken

1 lb fresh crabmeat

1 12 oz container fresh oysters, with juices (optional)

Hot cooked rice

Gumbo file

Combine ½ cup oil and the flour in a large pot. This is how you make the wonderful brown roux that is the base for the gumbo. Cook over medium heat, stirring constantly. When roux starts to look the color of caramel--about 20 minutes—stir in the celery, onion, green pepper and garlic and cook about 45 more minutes. You need to stir pretty regularly. You don't want anything to burn or stick.

Fry the okra in a tbsp of hot oil until browned. Add it to the emerging gumbo and and stir well over low heat for about five minutes. Now, if you need to, the mixture can be cooled and refrigerated—or even frozen—for later use. But at our house, when we start smelling the gumbo cooking, ain't nobody going nowhere until it is ready to put on the table. And then we shore ain't going nowhere.

Add broth and the next 11 ingredients and simmer 2 ½ to 3 hours in low, stirring from time to time. The last step is to peel and devein the shrimp and add the good stuff—the shrimp, chicken, crabmeat, and oysters. Do this during the last ten minutes of simmering. Remove the bay leaf, which is good for flavoring, but not eating. Serve over rice and sprinkle with gumbo file, if desired.

Makes about a dozen healthy cups

Chicken Mexican Soup

3 chicken breasts

2 tbsp olive oil

1 onion, chopped

2 cloves garlic, minced

3 cups chicken broth

1 can Rotel Tomatoes

1 can diced tomatoes

1 can black beans, rinsed and drained

1 can corn

2 tsp chili powder

½ tsp cayenne pepper

1 tsp cumin

1 tbsp cilantro

salt and pepper

Cut the chicken breasts into strips and sauté in olive oil, seasoning with salt and pepper. Remove the chicken and allow to drain. Cut into small pieces. Add the onions and garlic to the same pan and sauté until tender.

In a large pot, add all ingredients and seasonings, stirring constantly to mix. Simmer over low heat for 45-60 minutes and serve with tortilla strips and sour cream. Can be doubled for crowd and works great in crock pot.

Makes 6 servings

Cold Night Vegetable Soup

When The Hawk is out and there is a nip in the air—maybe it's even a little damp and rainy—nothing hits the spot like a bowl of hot vegetable soup. Unless, of course, it's another bowl. My mama used to put up tomatoes all summer and "soup mixture," which included corn and peas and okra and beans and I'm not sure what else. But I know that when she combined the two, along with whatever spices she used, and cooked a pan of hot cornbread—we had something fit to eat at our house.

You may or may not put soup mixture and tomatoes—and if you do, you probably already have your own vegetable soup recipe. Here's one that ain't bad and you can make do with canned tomatoes and frozen vegetables.

1 lb beef with bone (or substitute ground beef)

1 ½ tbsp oil

2 cups water

1 medium onion, chopped

1 cup sliced carrots

1 cup celery, chopped

2 cans tomatoes

1 bay leaf (remove before serving)

3 peppercorns

1 tbsp salt

2 tsp black pepper

½ tsp red pepper

1 tsp Tabasco sauce

1 cup whole kernel corn

1 cup sliced okra

½ cup fresh lima beans

Cut the beef off the bone and cut into small chunks. Brown the beef in oil in a large pot.   Add the water and the bone to the pot. Bring to a boil and then lower heat and simmer for an hour or so. Add the tomatoes and vegetables and seasonings and continue to simmer for another hour, until flavors are blended and vegetables are tender.

Makes 6 servings

Hard Times Potato Soup

My daddy used to talk about the "Hard Times" of the 1920s and 30s. He would lament about the days when a hot bowl of potato soup was a luxury. This recipe still tastes pretty luxurious to me.

4 russet potatoes

½ cup onions, chopped

½ cup celery, chopped

2 cans chicken broth

1 cup water

1 cup milk

2 tbsp butter

Peel and dice the potatoes. Peel and dice the onions and celery. Combine the broth and water and heat. Cook vegetables in the liquid until soft and tender. Add the butter, milk and seasonings. Simmer for about 30 minutes over low heat, stirring often.

Makes 8 servings

"If you want to hear a sad story, ask me about the price of cotton!"

DTH

Lisa's Special Ham-Bean Soup

Great use of left-over ham, with bone

1 16 oz pkg 15 bean soup mix

2 qts water

1 ham hock

1 (16 oz) can whole tomatoes, undrained and chopped

1 ½ cup chopped onions

3 tbsp lemon juice

1 green bell pepper, finely chopped

1 hot finger pepper, seeds removes, thinly sliced

1 tsp minced garlic

1 ¼ tsp salt

¼ tsp black pepper

1 tbsp Tabasco sauce

Wash the beans in a colander and sort through, picking out any bad looking beans. The last thing you want is a bad looking bean in a bowl of soup. Place the beans in a large pot of water and soak for 8 hours— or overnight.

Drain the beans and return to the big pot. Add 2 qts water and the ham hock. Bring to a boil, then cover and reduce heat to a simmer. Cook for about an hour-and-a-half. Remove ham from bone and chop meat and return to pot. Stir in the tomatoes, onions, lemon juice, peppers, garlic and seasonings. Bring the soup back to a boil and then reduce heat and simmer for another 30 minutes. Add additional salt and pepper to taste. This recipe works well in crock pot all day, also.

Beef Stew

2 lbs lean beef, cubed

2 tbsp oil

1 tsp Lawry's Seasoned Salt

½ tsp onion powder

½ tsp garlic powder

1 tbsp Worcestershire sauce

1 bay leaf

4 carrots, sliced

4 potatoes, cubed

1 large onion, cut into eighths

salt and pepper

In a large skillet, brown the beef in the oil and then cover with water. Add the seasoning and cover. Simmer for about 2 hours. Add the vegetables and simmer for another 30-45 minutes, until vegetables are tender.

Makes 6 serving

Good, better, best; never let it rest--'til the good get better and the better get best!

Brandy Woods Trail Five-Alarm Chili

After Lisa and I were married, our first home that was not a trailer was a wonderful little three-bedroom house that Cindy Head Jackson sold us on Brandy Woods Trail in Conyers. One of the first things we learned to make for company was chili. It was pretty cheap and pretty uncomplicated. One weekend our friends from Valdosta, Ken and Beth Cooper, were up for a visit and Lisa prepared the chili. Ken Cooper took one bite of that chili and sweat broke out all over his forehead. Ever the gentleman, Ken emptied his bowl and asked for seconds. But he also drank a gallon of tea and I am pretty sure he wet the bed that night. We have cut down on the hot stuff for this recipe.

2 lbs ground beef

1 tbsp butter

2 cans diced tomatoes

1 can Rotel tomatoes

2 tbsp chili powder

2 tbsp dry mustard

2 medium onions, chopped

2 cans chili hot beans

1 tbsp salt

1 tbsp pepper

1 tsp red pepper

1 tbsp Tabasco sauce

Brown the beef in the butter. Add all ingredients in a large pot. Bring to a boil and lower heat. Simmer for 1 ½ hours. Eat with cornbread, sliced onions and red peppers—at your own risk.

Now the Salads!

Chicken Salad

This is another dish that my mama made that I adored—and my lovely wife Lisa's tastes just like hers.

> **3 chicken breasts**
>
> **1-2 ribs of celery**
>
> **3 tbsp sweet salad cubes**
>
> **¼ cup chopped pecans**
>
> **½ cup mayonnaise**
>
> **½ tsp celery salt**
>
> **1 tsp salt**
>
> **black pepper**

Boil the chicken breasts until done throughout—about 25-30 minutes. Allow to cool. Shred chicken in a food processor. Finely chop the celery and nuts and add all the ingredients together. Add mayonnaise a little at a time until you reach the desired consistency. Add salt and pepper to taste.

Makes GREAT sandwiches!

Chicken and Grapes Pasta Salad

Carol Ingle taught Lisa how to make this recipe and if Carol Ingle has anything at all to do with it, it is first class—and you can take that directly to the bank.

2 cups shell macaroni

3 cups cooked and cubed chicken

¼ cup finely chopped onion

1 11 oz can of Mandarin oranges, drained

¾ cup slivered almonds, toasted

1 tsp salt

¼ cup diced celery

1 ½ cup seedless red grapes

1 ½ cup mayonnaise

3 tbsp fresh parsley, finely chopped

Cook the macaroni according to the package directions. Drain and rinse in cold water. In a large bowl, combine the pasta and the remaining ingredients. Cover and refrigerate 3 to 4 hours or overnight.

Sometimes you get the bear and sometimes the bear gets you.

JRB, Jr.

Aunt Renee's Classic Eight-Layer Salad

Most families have that one dish that they just have to serve at every special occasion. This is one of ours.

1 head lettuce

1 cup chopped celery

1 cup chopped bell pepper

1 cup chopped onion (purple or green onions)

1 pkg frozen English peas

1 can sliced water chestnuts, drained

1 ½ cups mayonnaise

2 tbsp sugar

1 cup grated cheddar cheese

6-10 strips bacon, fried and crumbled

Tear the lettuce into bite-sized pieces and place in a large clear bowl. Add the other vegetables and the cheese in alternating layers. Do not toss. Combine the sugar and mayonnaise and mix well. Spread the mayonnaise mixture over the top of the salad, sealing the edges. Cover tightly and refrigerate for at least 6 hours. When ready to serve, sprinkle the crumbled bacon over the top. This salad is even better when made a day in advance.

Serves 10—12

Strawberry Pretzel Salad

This was my mama's recipe. Lisa does it proud and it is always a treat. Feel free to make it your own.

2 ¾ cups pretzels, crushed

1 ½ stick butter, melted

8 oz cream cheese

1 cup sugar

2 cups Cool Whip

1 box strawberry Jello

2 cups hot water

2 10 oz pkgs frozen strawberries, defrosted

1 can crushed pineapple, drained (optional)

Crush the pretzels and mix with the melted butter. Cover the bottom of a greased 9x13 casserole dish with the mixture. Bake at 350 for 10 minutes. Allow to cool. Mix the cream cheese, sugar and Cool Whip. Spread over the pretzels and refrigerate.

Mix the Jello in boiling water until dissolved. Add the strawberries and pineapple in a bowl and place in refrigerator until partially set. Pour the mixture over second layer and refrigerate until completely set.

Makes 16 servings

Darrell's Special Coleslaw

1 pkg shredded coleslaw mix (lettuce and carrots)

¼ cup minced onions

½ cup sweet pickle salad cubes

½ cup mayonnaise

½ cup sour cream

¼ cup ranch dressing

2 tbsp vinegar

1 tsp celery seeds

1 tbsp sugar

salt and pepper

Pour the slaw mix into a big bowl. Leave plenty of room. Add the onions and salad cubes and stir. In a smaller bowl, mix all the other ingredients, making sure ingredients are well blended. Pour over the cabbage, making sure you scrape the bowl to get it all out. Stir to coat. Refrigerate at least an hour before serving.

Feeds 8-10

Vin-e-cumbers

One of the kids tried to ask for vinegar and cucumbers one day and this is how it came out. It's something good to have out when you are lucky enough to be having a meat and three type meal—and it is better the second day.

2 medium cucumbers

1 onion

1 cup apple cider vinegar

salt and pepper

Peel the cucumbers and cut into ¼ inch slices. Peel the onion and cut into eighths. Sprinkle salt and pepper liberally over the vegetables and cover with vinegar. Leave at room temperature for a couple of hours before serving.

Porterdale Pineapple Salad

When we first got married, Lisa ridiculed me for wanting to serve this, but it was at every covered dish dinner I ever went to coming up. And for the record, I still get invited to speak at a lot of church socials and there are still a lot of salt-of-the-earth people who still have the good sense to bring this salad. And for the record—it works well with pears, too.

12 canned pineapple slices

12 small gobs mayonnaise

½ head lettuce

6 cherries, cut in half

1 cup grated cheddar cheese

Cover a large serving tray with lettuce leaves, which have been washed and dried. Arrange the pineapple slices on top of the lettuce. Place a small gob of mayonnaise in the center of each. Cover with cheese and place half a cherry in the center of each pineapple slice.

Makes 12 servings

Orange Salad

Karen Tanner is not only a tremendous pianist, she is also a very talented teacher who did wonders with our youngest child, Jenna. She is a great cook, too. Ask any youth who has ever been on a summer trip with her. This is her recipe.

3 oz pkg orange Jello

1 small can crushed pineapple

1 cup grated cheddar cheese

½ cup chopped pecans

1 small container Cool Whip

Mix hot water with the Jello, according to pkg directions. Add the pineapple and let it thicken. Add the other ingredients and chill until ready to serve.

8-10 servings

Cranberry Salad

This is a classic.

1 8 oz can crushed pineapple—in juice, not syrup

2 tbsp lemon juice

1 3 oz pkg raspberry Jello

1 16 oz can whole cranberry sauce

½ cup celery, chopped

½ cup pecans, chopped

Drain the pineapple and save the juice. Cook the juice with the lemon and ½ cup of water. Heat to a boil, then remove from heat and add the Jello. Break up the cranberries and add to the gelatin mixture. Place in refrigerator and allow to partially set. Remove from the refrigerator and mix in the celery and pecans. Chill overnight and serve on lettuce.

Serves 8-10

Congealed Lime Salad

1 3 oz pkg lime Jello

1 3 oz pkg lemon Jello

2 cups hot water

1 cup mayonnaise

1 lg pkg cream cheese

1 small can crushed pineapple, drained

1 cup cold water

1 cup chopped pecans

Dissolve Jello in hot water. Blend the mayonnaise and cream cheese together. Add to the Jello mix, blending well. Add the pineapple and cold water, blending well. Stir in the pecans. Pour into an 8x12 Pyrex dish and refrigerate until firm.

8-10 servings

Tuna Salad

Last, but not least—well, maybe it is least. I guess it depends on whether you like tuna salad. I do.

1 small can Chicken of the Sea or StarKist tuna (Sorry, Charlie)

1 boiled egg, chopped

1 tbsp salad cubes

2 tbsp mayonnaise

salt and pepper

Mix everything together. Great on crackers or between two slices of white bread.

Makes 2-3 sandwiches, depending

Let's not forget the snacks!

BLT Dip

This stuff will disappear quicker than a tight-wad when the check comes!

1 lb bacon, cooked and crumbled

2 tomatoes, finely chopped

1 cup mayonnaise

1 cup sour cream

Cook the bacon and chop or crumble into small bits. Dice two small tomatoes into small cubes. Add the mayonnaise and sour cream. Mix well and serve with Fritos—the big ones that are made for scooping. Everyone will want to know who brought this dish and how to make it. Tell 'em just to buy a book!

Pimento Cheese the Martha Mann Way

What? You thought we were going to put out a Southern cookbook and not include a pimento cheese recipe? You can, of course, make sandwiches with this most excellent spread. We like to serve it as an appetizer, with Club Crackers. It is also great spread on celery sticks. Use it as you see fit, but don't pass it up—even if you think you don't like pimento cheese.

3 cups sharp cheddar cheese, grated

4 oz jar diced pimentos

Blue Plate mayonnaise to blend

Beat the cheese and pimentos, slowly adding mayonnaise until you reach the desired consistency. You might want to sprinkle a little salt into the mix as you go.

Bread Bowl Dip

Now this here dish is real good for putting in one of them scooped out bread bowls, if you are trying to have a fancy party.

1 8 oz pkg cream cheese (softened)

1 pkg Buddig dried beef, finely chopped

½ cup sour cream

½ cup minced onions

2 tsp chopped bell pepper

½ cup chopped walnuts (or pecans)

salt and pepper

Mix all ingredients well. Chill and serve in bread bowl.

Standard Spinach Dip

Yeah, I didn't think I liked spinach either until I started eating this stuff. Bluto wouldn't have stood a chance if Olive Oyl had made this recipe for Popeye.

1 cup sour cream

1 cup mayonnaise

1 pkg Knox vegetable soup mix

1 10 oz pkg frozen chopped spinach, thawed and drained

1 8 oz can water chestnuts, drained and chopped

1 medium onion, finely chopped

Blend all ingredients in a blender or food processor. Chill at least 8 hours. Serve in hollowed out pumpernickel bread loaf or in a bowl with crackers or raw vegetables.

Baked Onion Dip

1 cup sliced Vidalia onions

1 cup grated Parmesan cheese (may substitute shredded Swiss)

1 cup mayonnaise

1 clove garlic

1 tsp Tabasco sauce

Combine all ingredients and pour into a shallow Pyrex baking dish. Bake at 375 for 25 minutes, or until brown. Serve with dipper chips.

Bacon Wraps

1 box of Waverly Club Wafers

1 16 oz block cream cheese

1 lb lean bacon

Cut each slice of bacon in half. Put one thin slice of cream cheese between 2 Waverly Wafers. Wrap in a half slice of bacon. Bake at 425 (seam side down) for 10 to 15 minutes. Turn over and bake an additional 10 minutes.

Makes 40 servings

900 Miles South of Buffalo Wings

You can't have a Super Bowl party without wings. They may have originated in Buffalo, but I have made these my own.

4 lbs chicken wings, separated at the joint

1 stick butter, melted

6 tbsp Tabasco sauce

4 tsp paprika

½ tsp salt

½ tsp black pepper

½ tsp red pepper

1 tbsp Worcestershire sauce

Cut the tips off the wings and separate at the joints. Place the wings in a gallon-size freezer bag and set aside. (You may need two bags. If so, split the marinade evenly between the two.) Melt the butter and add the Tabasco, paprika, salt, pepper and Worcestershire sauce. Mix well and pour over chicken.

Marinate the wings for about half an hour and then remove the wings. Place the wings on a broiler pan covered with non-stick foil. Broil 4-5 inches from the heat source for about 20-25 minutes, turning once at the midpoint of the cooking time. Serve with favorite dressing and celery sticks.

An alternative way of cooking the wings is to marinate them and then cook on a hot grill, basting with the reserve marinade—after you have brought it to a boil in the microwave.

Another alternative is to deep fry the wings and then pour the marinade over them. Have plenty of napkins ready no matter what method you choose.

Redneck Caviar

Everybody has their own version. This is how my daughter, Dr. Jamie, makes it.

2 cans Rotel Diced Tomatoes

2 cans diced tomatoes, drained

2 cans black-eyed peas, rinsed and drained

12 green onions, chopped

1 green bell pepper, chopped

1 Vidalia onion, chopped

½ bunch parsley chopped

1 tbsp garlic powder

1 tbsp salt

16 oz Zesty Italian salad dressing

¼ cup lime juice

Mix it all together and set it out with some Frito scoops or your favorite tortilla chips—or, better yet, pork rinds.

Never let the truth stand in the way of a good story.

Huckism

Party Meatballs

2 1 lb bags frozen pre-cooked cocktail size meatballs

1 16 oz can jellied cranberry sauce

1 12 oz bottle chili sauce

1 tsp cumin

¼ tsp cayenne pepper

Combine the sauces and cook over medium-low heat, stirring until smooth. Add the meatballs and stir. Cook about 15 more minutes, until meatballs are heated through.

Makes 30 appetizer sized servings

Cajun Crab Dip

¼ lb cream cheese, softened

½ cup sour cream

1 tsp Worcestershire sauce

¼ tsp minced garlic

1 small Vidalia onion, finely chopped

½ bunch parsley, finely chopped

1 tsp red pepper

1 tsp Tabasco sauce

¼ cup Half-and-Half

½ tsp salt

½ tsp black pepper

1 lb lump crab meat, cooked

Pour all the ingredients except the actual crab meat into a large bowl. Carefully add the crab meat, stirring gently. Pour into a shallow Pyrex baking dish and cook at 350 for about 20 minutes. Serve with crackers. For a real treat, serve with a few raw oysters on the half shell. This delectable treat can also be served cold.

Now turn out the lights; the party's over.

Save Room for

Dessert!

The Sweet Stuff

You've heard that old expression—we've saved the best for last? Well they don't call it dessert for nothing you know. I didn't have that much of a sweet tooth when I was coming up. My mama cooked a meat, three vegetables and homemade bread seven out of seven days, but she wasn't one for baking. I guess that's why I didn't develop a craving for cakes and pies and such until later in life.

Well trust me, boys and girls, I have more than made up for it since. I love cake—especially my sister's German chocolate cake. I love pies—especially pecan and coconut and sweet potato. I love custards and cheese cakes and homemade ice cream.

Let me tell you—the Huckaby family likes to make ice cream. Peach is our specialty, but we make vanilla and strawberry and chocolate and lime sherbet and . . .

Well, I know what you are thinking right now. Quit talking about it and let me get to the recipes. Here they are—all sorts of delectable cobblers and confections. And there's not a single calorie in the entire chapter. There are lots and lots of calories in the food, if you actually cook it—but none in the chapter itself.

Enjoy, y'all. We only live once.

Myron's German Chocolate Cake

German chocolate is, without a doubt, my very favorite cake. And my sister, Myron Singley, makes the very best in the world. Hands down. Sometimes she will make me one for my birthday or Christmas and bring it to me while it is still warm. You don't know what good is until you've had a piece of my sister's German chocolate cake, fresh out of the oven, with a big glass of cold milk. Trust me on this one. It is worth the effort.

    ½ cup boiling water

    2 ½ cups flour

    1 square German Chocolate

    ¼ teaspoon salt

    2 sticks Parkay margarine

    1 tsp baking soda

    2 cups sugar

    1 cup buttermilk

    4 egg yolks, beaten

    4 egg whites, beaten stiffly

    1 tsp vanilla

Melt chocolate in water. Set aside to cool. Cream margarine and sugar until light and fluffy. Add well-beaten egg yolks one at a time. Add vanilla and chocolate. Mix well. Sift together flour, salt and soda. Add alternately to margarine mixture, the dry ingredients and the buttermilk Beat thoroughly. Fold in stiffly beaten egg whites. Pour into 3 greased and floured 8 or 9 inch cake pans. Bake 35 to 40 minutes at 350 degrees. Cool. Frost between layers and on top with Coconut-Pecan Frosting.

Frosting

    4 egg yolks

    1 12 oz can evaporated milk

    1 ½ tsp vanilla

1 ½ cups sugar

1 ½ sticks margarine

7 oz Baker's Angel Flake coconut

1 ½ chopped Pecans

Beat egg yolks, milk and vanilla in large saucepan with whisk until well blended. Add sugar and butter. Cook on medium heat 12 min., or until thickened and golden brown. Stir constantly. remove from heat Add coconut and nuts. Mix well. Cool. Spread on German Chocolate Cake.

Pecan Pie

Now I already maligned my mama by saying that she didn't bake. She made an exception at Christmas and the thing she made the best was pecan pie. We all know that pecan pie is as Southern as it gets. This recipe is not my mama's. It is Cassie Potts's recipe. She is Lisa's aunt. But it tastes just like mama's—and that is about as high praise as this old linthead boy can dish out.

1 cup white Karo syrup

3 eggs

1 ½ cup chopped pecans

½ cup sugar

1 stick butter

1 tsp vanilla

2 regular Pet Ritz pie shells

Place the pecans in the bottom of the unbaked pie shells. Mix the Karo syrup, sugar and eggs together. Make sure they are well mixed. Melt the butter and add to the mixture, along with the vanilla. Pour the mixture over the pecans in the two shells. Place in a 400 degree oven and bake 10 minutes. Reduce to 300 degrees and continue baking 25 minutes, until golden brown. As soon as they are done you will see

185

why we told you to go ahead and make two. Serve with ice cream or whipped cream or as is and give thanks that you at least know someone raised in the American South.

Lorie Scroggs's Red Velvet Cake

Lorie Scroggs is one of my favorite people, even if her husband Craig doesn't bring much luck with him when he comes to watch a football game on TV. Lorie is a real peach from deep South Georgia, way below the gnat line. She is in my Sunday school class and whenever we can get her to make her Red Velvet cake for a special event—well, shoot fire—if she makes her Red Velvet cake the event is automatically special. And she has been kind enough to share her recipe with all of us.

2 ½ cups self-rising flour

1 ½ cups sugar

1 cup buttermilk

1 tsp unsweetened cocoa powder

1 ½ cups vegetable oil

1 tsp white vinegar

1 tsp baking soda

2 large eggs

1 tsp vanilla extract

2 oz red food coloring

(Lorie only uses 1 oz of food coloring. She likes the color better.)

Preheat the oven to 350. Mix together all the ingredients with an electric mixer. Spray three 9 inch round cake pans with Pam. Pour the batter equally into the pans and bake for 22 minutes. Test for doneness with a toothpick. Cool the layers in the pans, on a wire rack for 10 minutes. Carefully remove layers from the pans to the racks to cool completely. Add the frosting.

Frosting

> **1/3 lb butter, softened**
>
> **10 oz cream cheese, softened**
>
> **1 lb box confectioner's sugar**
>
> **2 cups chopped pecans**

Combine the butter, cream cheese and confectioner's sugar in a bowl. Beat until fluffy, then fold in 1 ½ cups of pecans. Use to fill and frost cake when it is cool. Decorate with the remaining ½ cup of pecans. Refrigerate for at least one hour before serving. (Lorie admits that she likes to double the frosting recipe and really pile it on.)

Italian Cream Cake

This might be the King of Cakes. We got our recipe from Grandmama Bitzi. I think she stole it from Carolyn Mouchette, whose husband Roland was the first band director at Heritage High School—where all our kids were bandos. Roland started a grand tradition that continues to this day—and so did Carolyn.

> **1 cup buttermilk**
>
> **½ cup Crisco**
>
> **1 tsp soda**
>
> **2 cups all purpose flour**
>
> **5 eggs, separated**

1 tsp vanilla

2 cups sugar

1 cup pecans, chopped

1 stick margarine

1 can coconut

Beat the egg whites until stiff. Combine the soda and buttermilk and let stand. Cream the margarine, sugar and Crisco. Add the egg yolks, one at a time, and beat. Alternate flour and buttermilk and add the vanilla. Add the egg whites and mix. Add the coconut and the pecans. Bake at 325 for 25 minutes, or until done.

Makes 3 layers

Frosting

8 oz cream cheese

1 box 4X sugar

1 stick margarine

1 tsp vanilla

Mix all ingredients together until smooth. Frost the cake after it is cooled. Sprinkle with a few chopped pecans on top for decoration.

Peach Cobbler

You just can't get more Southern than this. And although this recipe calls for peaches, you can make it with apples or blackberries—I love it with blackberries—or any combination thereof. My lovely wife, Lisa, messes it up from time to time by adding blueberries. But if you like blueberries, I guess that works, too.

1 cup self-rising flour

1 cup sugar

¾ cup milk

1 stick butter

3 cups fruit

Melt the butter in a casserole dish. Mix the flour, sugar and milk together. Pour into the casserole dish over the melted butter. DO NOT STIR. (My mother-in-law put that in big letters because you really don't need to stir.) Add 3 cups of your favorite fruit (canned is acceptable) and—again—DO NOT STIR. Cook at 350 for about 40-45 minutes, until golden brown. Serve with vanilla ice cream and you'll want to slap your granny it's so good!

Joan McMullan's Magnificent Banana Pudding

For the past decade or so the Huckaby clan has been embraced by a wonderful group of people called the Oak Tree Tailgate Gang. On autumn Saturdays, when the Georgia Bulldogs tee it up between the hedges, the members of the Oak Tree Gang—elders, acorns and sprouts—gather at the top of the hill behind the Veterinary Sciences Building—more commonly known as the Vet School—to relive past glories, revel in the pomp and circumstance that is Southern college football and—of course, eat. Wheeler Davidson, the Self-Appointed, Non-Elected and Can't-be-fired Chairman Emeritus of the Oak Tree Gang announces every weekend that "no one does Georgia football with a more beautiful group of women" than we do. And he is absolutely correct. He and his cohort, Dan Ragsdale, arrive in Athens with the sun and make everything ready for the rest of us—and I am firmly convinced that it is not pure altruism that motivates them. I think they keep returning to tailgate beneath the oak trees year after year after year, at least in large part, because of Joan McMullan's banana pudding. It is as much a staple of our gatherings as Wheeler's Bloody Marys. She claims she got the recipe off a Nabisco 'Nilla Wafers box—but she has a special touch the people who printed that box cannot approach. Give it a try and see what kind of touch you have.

¾ cup sugar

3 eggs, separated

2 tbsp flour

Nilla Vanilla Wafers

¼ tsp salt

2 cups milk

6 medium size ripe bananas, sliced

Combine ½ cup sugar, flour and salt in the top of double boiler. Stir in the milk. Cook in the double boiler, over boiling water, stirring constantly, until thickened. Cook, uncovered, 15 minutes more, stirring occasionally. Beat egg yolks. Gradually stir in some of the hot mixture into the eggs. Then add the eggs to the mixture in the double boiler. Cook 5 minutes, stirring constantly. Remove from heat.

Line bottom of a 1½ quart casserole with 'Nilla Wafers. Top with a layer of sliced bananas. Pour a portion of custard over the bananas. Continue to layer wafers, bananas and custard ending with custard on top.

Beat the egg whites stiff, but not dry. Gradually add the remaining ¼ cup sugar and beat until mixture forms stiff peaks. Pile on top of pudding in casserole. Bake in a preheated hot oven at 425 for 5 minutes, or until delicately browned. Serve warm or chilled.

Makes 6 servings, so I'm pretty sure Joan triples it on Game Day.

Strawberry Cake

1 box of Duncan Hines white cake mix

1 small box strawberry Jello

1 cup oil

4 eggs

1 cup frozen strawberries (thawed & drained)

Mix cake mix and Jello together. Add the oil and beat well. Add the eggs, one at a time, beating after each. Add the strawberries and blend well. Pour into greased and floured cake pans. Bake in 3 layers at 350 for 25 to 35 minutes or until done. (Don't overcook.) Remove from cake pans after 10 mins. Place on wire racks to cool. Let cake get completely cool before icing.

Strawberry Icing

1 box 4X confectioners' sugar

1 stick margarine

¼ to ½ cup frozen strawberries

Beat the margarine until softened. Put all sugar in a bowl. Add the strawberries a little at a time, beating as you add them, until you get the consistency you want.

(If you add too many strawberries, your icing will run off the cake!)

Muscadine Pie

Yes, you can make a pie out of grapes. This recipe is from Mary Anne Gordon who teaches how to make jelly in a previous chapter. I think you get the idea. The gal likes scuppernongs!

2 ½ cups muscadines or scuppernongs

3 tbsp melted butter

1 cup sugar

2 tbsp flour

homemade or store-bought pie crust

Wash the grapes and separate fruit pulp from hulls. Press fruit pulp through strainer or sieve to remove all seeds. Combine pulp and hulls in heavy saucepan or Dutch oven. Boil until hulls are tender. Remove from heat and add butter, sugar, and flour. Pour into well-greased pie pan. Place crust on top. Cut strips in crust or insert ceramic pie bird to vent. Bake at 425 degrees for 25-30 minutes, until crust is brown and pie filling is bubbly. Allow to cool for 15 minutes before serving. Top with vanilla ice cream if desired.

Toll House Cookies

My mother-in-law, Bitzi Potts, makes these when we go camping at Jekyll Island in the spring and at Christmas and sometimes just to be making them. She was a Cowan and they are from a secret Cowan family recipe—so shhhh!

1 ½ cup plain flour, sifted

1 cup butter

¾ cup sugar

¾ cup brown sugar

2 eggs

1 tsp hot water

1 tsp soda

1 tsp vanilla

2 cups Quaker Oats

1 cup pecans, chopped

1 16 oz pkg semi-sweet chocolate chips

Cream the butter until soft and add sugar gradually until you get a creamy texture. Add eggs, one at a time. Dissolve the soda in water and add to mix. Mix in flour, salt and vanilla—and then the oats. Add nuts and fold in the chocolate chips. Place 1 tsp size balls on a cookie sheet and bake at 325 until done—about 8-10 minutes. Remove and cool on a wire rack.

Makes 8 dozen cookies

Strawberry Pie

Or as Jackson calls it—breakfast. This makes 2 pies. One for Jackson and one for everyone else.

2 frozen pie shells

1 ½ cup sugar

1 ½ cup water

5 tbsp cornstarch

5 tbsp strawberry Jello

Mix water, sugar and cornstarch over medium heat until clear and thick. Remove from heat and add Jello and stir. Cool in the refrigerator. Bake the pie shell per directions on pkg. When cool, place a layer of whole strawberries in each shell. (You may prefer to use strawberries that have been cut in half.) Pour the glaze over to cover and refrigerate until set. You'll swear you are back at Shoney's—only better. Top it with Cool Whip and it is better still.

Each pie makes 6 servings, for regular folks

Cream Cheese Pound Cake

Lord have mercy, we are getting serious now. This is Renee Marrett's recipe and if you are only going to have one pound cake recipe, this is the one to have.

1 **8 oz pkg cream cheese**

3 **sticks butter**

3 **cups sugar**

3 **cups sifted plain flour**

6 **eggs**

2 **tbsp vanilla**

Cream the butter and cheese until fluffy. Add the sugar and beat— again—until fluffy. Add the flour, alternating with the eggs, and mix well. Add the vanilla last. Pour the batter into a well greased and floured Bundt pan and bake at 300 for 1 hour and 20 minutes. Turn onto a rack and allow to cool.

Martha Mann's Coconut Cake

We getting more Southern by the minute, y'all.

1 **cup Crisco**

2 **cups sugar**

3 **cups self-rising flour**

4 **eggs**

1 **tsp vanilla**

1 **cup buttermilk**

¼ **cup water**

194

Mix the Crisco, sugar and eggs and then slowly add the flour, milk and water. Rub the pans with shortening and dust with flour. Pour into 4 pans and bake for 28-30 minutes at 325.

7 Minute Frosting

> **3 egg whites, unbeaten**
>
> **7 ½ tbsp cold water**
>
> **2 ¼ cups sugar**
>
> **1 ½ tsp corn syrup—light**
>
> **1 large pkg flaked coconut**

Put all the ingredients except the vanilla in the top of a double boiler. Beat for about 7 minutes—thus the name—and then remove and add vanilla. Spread on cool cake layer and top with coconut—frozen or canned.

Lagniappe

Down New Orleans way, folks are familiar with the term "lagniappe." It means "a little something extra," like when you order a dozen dough-nuts and the baker gives you thirteen. Martha has included a little something extra in her cake recipe.

> **1 cup milk**
>
> **2 tbsp butter**
>
> **1/3 cup sugar**

Combine all ingredients and bring to a boil. On each cake layer, just before you put on the icing, take a big spoon and spread some of the mixture over each layer. It makes the cake good and moist!

Sweet Potato Pie

My lovely wife, Lisa, makes pumpkin pies. If you want a recipe for a good pumpkin pie, check out the Yankee Eatin' Cookbook. I was raised eating sweet potato pie and this is how my mama made hers.

4 oz butter, softened

2 cups mashed up sweet potatoes

2 cups sugar

1 small can evaporated milk

1 tsp vanilla

3 eggs

2 unbaked store-bought pie shells

Boil the potatoes until done, then peel them and mash them up real good. Mix the butter, sugar and milk together until everything is nice and smooth. Beat the eggs and add the eggs and vanilla. (If you just have to add a tsp of cinnamon go ahead. I prefer mine without. I'm just funny that way.) Pour it all into a prepared pie shell and bake at 350 for about an hour.

Makes 6 servings—so you'd best double the recipe and make 2

Mississippi Mud

1 cup chopped nuts

3 tbsp cocoa

1 ½ stick butter

1 ½ cup sugar

3 eggs

1 ½ cup self-rising flour

Cream the butter and add cocoa to sugar and sift. Add eggs, one at a time, then the flour and nuts. Pour in greased and floured baking dish and cook 40 minutes at 350.

Icing

1 box 4x sugar, softened

4 tbsp cocoa

4 tbsp butter

¼ tsp salt

4 tbsp milk

2 tbsp hot coffee

1 tsp vanilla

½ cup mini-marshmallows

Cream the butter and add the cocoa. Add sugar, salt, milk, coffee and vanilla and beat until smooth. When the cake is done, place ½ cup of miniature marshmallows on the cake. Pour the icing on top of the marshmallows. Allow to sit for at least five hours before cutting. This cake mellows with age. It is much better the second day.

Crustless Brownie Pie

1 cup sugar

½ cup all purpose flour

¼ cup cocoa

½ cup butter, softened

2 eggs

1 tsp vanilla

pinch of salt

½ cup pecans

Combine the first 7 ingredients. Beat 4 minutes on medium speed with an electric mixer. Stir in the nuts. Spread butter evenly in a buttered 9 inch pie plate. Bake at 325 for 35 to 40 minutes or until a toothpick stuck in the center comes out clean. Serve with whipped cream or ice cream. Yummy!

Chess Pie

2 eggs

2 tbsp flour

1 cup sugar

1 tbsp cornmeal

½ cup milk

1 tsp vanilla

½ cup butter

Mix all ingredients in a large bowl. Pour into an unbaked pie shell and bake at 325 for 30 minutes.

Terry Lynn's Chocolate Cake

When Terry Lynn married into the family one of the many positives was that she brought her chocolate cake recipe with her. This is Jenna's favorite cake. The recipe makes two layers and uses a whipped cream frosting.

1 **cup brown sugar**

1 **pint whipping cream**

1 **cup pecans, chopped**

1 **box Devil's Food Cake Mix**

½ **cup butter**

confectioners' sugar

In a saucepan, mix 1 cup brown sugar, ½ cup butter, and ¼ cup whipping cream. Melt over low heat, stirring to avoid scorching. This makes a caramel glaze.

Mix the cake according to directions on the box.

Grease 2 cake pans and pour the glaze into the pans. Sprinkle the chopped pecans over the glaze in a single layer. Pour the cake mix slowly over the nuts. Bake at 325 for about 45 minutes. Take out of the oven and cool on wire racks for about 10 minutes. Make the whipping cream, adding a bit of confectioners' sugar to taste. Spread between layers and assemble.

Tommie's Fruitcake Cookies

It ain't Christmas at our house until somebody makes Tommie Hucka-by's fruitcake cookies. Luckily, Lisa is pretty good at it.

1 lb creamed butter

1 cup light brown sugar

1 cup white sugar

3 eggs

3 cups plain flour, divided

½ cup milk

1 tsp soda

1 tsp baking powder

1 tsp cinnamon

½ lb candied pineapple, cut into pieces

1 lb candied cherries, cut into pieces

2 cups dates, cut into pieces

8 cups coarsely chopped pecans

In a large bowl, dredge some flour into the fruit mixtures until coated and set aside. Cream the butter and add the sugar and then the eggs, well beaten. Sift the rest of the flour, the soda and the baking powder together. Add the flour and milk and then fold in the fruit mixture and pecans. Drop by spoonfuls onto a greased cookie sheet and bake at 300 for about 15-20 minutes, until the cookies are a light brown color. If the dough seems to spread too fast, put it in the refrigerator for a few minutes before dropping on pan.

Makes a gracious plenty for the Christmas season

Christmas Crescents

One of the joys of Christmas is to see Jamie and Jenna in the kitchen with their mama, aprons on and faces covered with flour—and smiles. These are among our favorite Christmas cookies.

2 sticks butter

2 cups plain flour

1 tsp vanilla

¾ cup confectioners' sugar

2 cups chopped pecans

1 cup 10X sugar

Cream the butter and add first the sugar and then the flour. (slowly) Add the vanilla and the pecans and mix well. Form into 1 inch balls and then press into crescent shapes. Place on a cookie sheet and bake at 300 for 20-25 minutes—until the cookies turn a very light golden brown color. Remove from the oven and take off the pan immediately. Roll the crescents in confectioners' sugar. (Putting them in a bag with the sugar and shaking is one way.)   Place on a wire rack to cool.

Makes 3-4 dozen cookies

It really 'tis the season once these are ready.

Brownies

I know. I know. You can just buy a mix. These are worth the extra effort. Promise.

1 cup sugar

2/3 cup flour

1/3 cup Crisco (It'll do you proud—every time.)

½ tsp baking powder

2 squares chocolate

¼ tsp salt

2 eggs, beaten

½ cup nuts, chopped

1 tsp vanilla

Sift the flour once. Measure the baking powder and salt and sift together. Melt the shortening and the chocolate over boiling water. Add the sugar gradually to the eggs, beating thoroughly. Add the shortening and chocolate mixture and stir to blend. Add the flour, nuts and vanilla. Bake in a greased pan (8x8x2) at 350 for about 35 minutes. Allow to cool for 10 minutes then cut into squares and enjoy with a big glass of cold milk.

Fresh Apple Cake

This is real good to make in the fall, when Ben Evans starts getting those crisp Georgia mountain apples in. Actually, it's pretty good any time.

1 1/8 cup Wesson Oil

3 cups plain flour (sifted 4-5 times)

2 cups sugar

1 tsp salt

3 eggs, well beaten

1 tsp baking soda

3 cups fresh apples, diced (small)

2 tsp vanilla

1 cup pecans, chopped

Mix all ingredients. Pour into a greased and floured pan. Bake at 325 for 35 minutes.

Icing

1 cup brown sugar

1 stick butter

¼ cup milk

1 tsp vanilla

Melt butter over low heat and add brown sugar, milk and vanilla. Bring to a boil. Pour over cooked cake while still warm.

Cherry Cheese Pie

1 9 inch Graham cracker crumb crust

8 oz cream cheese, softened

1 14 oz can Eagle brand condensed milk

1/3 cup lemon juice

1 tsp vanilla

1 can cherry pie filling

In a large mixing bowl, beat the cheese until fluffy. Beat in the Eagle brand milk until smooth. Stir in the lemon juice and vanilla. Pour into pie crust. Chill for 3 hours before serving.

Cherry Crunch

This stuff is so good with vanilla ice cream that it ought to be a sin. In fact, I am pretty sure it is! Thank goodness for grace!

1 can cherry pie filling

1 pkg yellow cake mix

½ cup chopped pecans

1 stick butter, melted

Spread the pie filling in the bottom of a 9x11 casserole dish and cover with the cake mix. Do not stir. Sprinkle the nuts on top and pour the melted butter over the top of the nuts. Bake at 350 for 30 minutes until golden brown.

Makes 6-8 servings

Ice Cream Time—Make mine homemade!

Every summer we do something called Camp Meeting. It's a Southern thing, y'all. Most of Lisa's family gathers in a little cabin we call a tent. There is a kitchen and a bathroom and several little sleeping cells with curtains instead of doors. The bathroom has an antique hot water heater and we live in constant fear—at least our cousin Kris and I do—that we'll forget to turn the water heater off when we go to sleep at night, causing the whole tent to explode. So far we've been lucky.

We go to church about three times a day during camp meeting, under a big open-air tabernacle. In between there is a lot of front porch sitting among the old folks and a lot of he-in' and she-in' among the young folks and a lot of eating by everybody.

Every evening, during camp meeting, we make ice cream at our tent. We make it the old fashioned way—with rock salt and a churn, although we did give in to modern conveniences and replace our old hand-turned freezers with electric models sometime during the 1970s. Every night, after evening services, you can find a long line of folks standing in the kitchen of our tent, waiting to be served a *Dixie* cup full of homemade ice cream.

After taps has sounded and the light-weight ice cream eaters have gone home, my good friend Daniel Farley arrives for his nightly ration. He and I sit and solve the problems of the world until his wife, Paige, tires of tending to an entire tent full of kids alone and comes to fetch him home. I try to keep Daniel talking as long as possible because Paige is one of my favorite people in the history of the world and about the only time I get to talk to her is when she comes looking for Daniel.

But I digress. We make a lot of different kinds of ice cream down at Salem. I have gotten permission to share five of the most popular flavors with you. All these recipes are for use with a four quart freezer. Increase accordingly for a 6 quart. If you can't do the math, call Daniel. He went to Georgia Tech, you know.

How to Freeze Ice Cream

No matter what kind of ice cream you are making, the freezing techniques are the same. Too many people miss out on a lot of fun—not to mention great eatin'—because they are afraid to use that freezer somebody gave them. It is really simple.

Just mix the ice cream according to the recipe. WARNING!!! None of the recipes that follow call for the mixture to be cooked before freezing. Using raw eggs in a recipe can be hazardous to your health, so if you want to be safe—use pasteurized eggs. Let me say that again. Using raw eggs in a recipe can be hazardous to your health, so if you want to be safe—use pasteurized eggs. Got that?

OK. Fill the canister of your ice cream freezer to the fill line. Place it in the bucket—don't forget the dasher—and connect the churn. Plug in the cord and add about a 3 inch layer of ice, followed by an inch or two of rock salt. Repeat the process until the freezer is full. Don't be stingy with the rock salt. It is the cheapest part of the recipe and speeds up the freezing process tremendously.

Monitor the freezer constantly, adding ice and rock salt as needed to keep the churn full. If you use enough ice and salt, the cream will usually freeze after about 20 minutes. When the motor stops turning, unplug and remove the dasher. If there isn't a kid around to lick it, do it yourself. Place a square of wax paper over the top of the canister and replace the lid. Pour off the brine, being careful not to let the water leak into the canister. Pack with ice and salt and cover with a towel. Let stand for an hour or two before serving.

Vanilla Ice Cream

I started to call this basic vanilla, but once you taste it, you'll know there is nothing basic about it.

5 eggs Pasteurized

1 large can evaporated milk

2 cups sugar

2 cups half-and-half

1 ½ tbsp vanilla

milk to take level to fill line (4-6 cups)

Beat the eggs with a mixer. Add the sugar, evaporated milk, vanilla and more milk, to fill the mixing bowl. Stir until well blended. Add to canister and add more milk—to fill line. (Feel free to use half-and-half instead of milk for creamier—and more fattening--ice cream.) Stir well and freeze using method described above.

Chocolate Ice Cream

Tastes just like a Frosty at that hamburger joint that is not Mickey D's.

1 qt Mayfield whole chocolate milk (or brand that is available)

1 large container of Cool Whip

1 14 oz can Eagle brand condensed milk

Just mix and freeze. Anybody can do it!

Lime Sherbet

2 cups boiling water

2 small lime Jello pkgs

2 cups sugar

½ cup freshly squeezed lime juice

½ cup freshly squeezed lemon juice

1 tsp lime zest

milk (2 %) to fill

Dissolve the Jello in the water. Add the sugar, juices and lime zest. Mix well. Add to the canister and fill to line with milk. Stir well, until blended. Freeze using method described above.

Strawberry Ice Cream

5 eggs Pasteurized

1 large can evaporated milk

1 ¾ -2 cups sugar (to taste)

2 cups half-and-half

4 cups chopped ripe strawberries (frozen strawberries work well, too)

½ tsp vanilla

milk to fill

Peel and finely chop the peaches. They need to be very ripe. Peaches bought at Evans Market are by far the best for this recipe. Put the chopped strawberries into a separate bowl. Beat the eggs in a mixer and add the sugar, evaporated milk, peaches and extracts. Mix well and pour into the canister. Then add the extra milk to the fill line. Freeze according to the directions above.

Perfection Personified Peach Ice Cream

Jackson Lee Huckaby claims credit for perfecting our family's peach ice cream recipe, and the great Methodist preacher, John Ed Mathison, can testify to Jackson's abilities. Once John Ed discovered our peach ice cream, he personally tried to get Salem Camp Meeting converted to a year round event. Here's how you do it.

5 eggs Pasteurized

1 large can evaporated milk

1 ¾ -2 cups sugar (to taste)

2 cups half-and-half

4 cups chopped RIPE peaches, mashed

1 tsp almond extract

¼ tsp vanilla

milk to fill

Peel and finely chop the peaches. They need to be very ripe. Peaches bought at Evans Market are by far the best for this recipe. Put the chopped peaches into a separate bowl. Beat the eggs in a mixer and add the sugar, evaporated milk, peaches and extracts. Mix well and pour into the canister. Then add the extra milk to the fill line. Freeze according to the directions above and when it is ready—call me and John Ed. We love us some of Jackson's peach ice cream!

Recipe Index

hushpuppies 120
pumpkin bars   36
sweet rolls   31
pecan waffles20
plain waffles 19

Cakes
apple 203
chocolate 199
coconut 194
coffee cake 34
German chocolate 184
Italian cream 187
pound 194
red velvet 186
strawberry 190

Casseroles
breakfast   21
broccoli and rice 150
chicken noodle 62
chicken stuffing   68
corn   93
ham and potato   74
hash brown potato 144
pizza 69
squash 91

Chicken
baked   64
barbecued   115
beer can   113
Buffalo wings 178
chicken breast on beef   64
chicken and dumplings   67
chicken Divan 146

okra, fried 86
onions, baked 93
pinto beans 87
potatoes, fried 96
potatoes, mashed 95
roasted new potatoes 153
squash, fried 90
squash, with onions 85
sweet potatoes, baked 94
sweet potato soufflé 151
sweet tea 103
turnip greens 81

Soups
beef stew 165
Brunswick stew 156
chicken Mexican 160
chicken stew 158
chili 166
gumbo 158
ham-bean 164
oyster stew 157
potato 163
vegetable 161

Turkey
smoked, 126, 131

Venison
loin, 132
roast, 132

About the Authors

Darrell Huckaby is a native of Porterdale, a North Georgia mill village, and a double graduate of the University of Georgia. His lovely wife, Lisa was born and raised ten miles down the road in Conyers, They met in the south Georgia town of Valdosta in the spring of 1981 and were married in December of 1982. They have three children, Jamie, Jackson, and Jenna- all University of Georgia students or graduates.

Darrell is a veteran educator with more than 37 years of classroom experience as of this writing. He is also an award winning newspaper columnist whose reflections on life in the American South have regaled his readers for many years. His first book, *Need Two*, was a regional best seller in 1995 and he has subsequently written eight other books, including *Grits is Groceries, Southern is as Southern Does, A Southener looks at All Fifty,* and *Dinner on the Grounds, the Ulimate Church Cookbook.* In his spare time, he travels across the South, speaking to church and civic groups and at corporate functions and sharing his particular brand of Southern wit and wisdom. He also does a weekly comedy spot on the *Moby in the Morning* country radio network. Cooking good Southern food is one of his many hobbies. Eating good Southern food is his passion.

Lisa Huckaby is a Certified Nurse Midwife and has helped bring more than 2500 babies into the world. She is a graduate of Valdosta State College and the Frontier School of Nurse Midwifery. She also holds a Masters degree in Nursing from Case Western Reserve in Cleveland Ohio. This is her first literary effort, but she has been cooking really good food for a long, long time.

Other Books by Darrell Huckaby

Need Two
Dinner on the Grounds
Grits is Groceries
Southern Is as Southern Does
Hard Rock to Solid Rock
Need Four
What the Huck
A Southerner Looks at all 50 States
Kelley's Boys

You may order copies of Darrell Huckaby's books at
www.darrellhuckaby.net

Book Darrell Huckaby as a Speaker!

If you are looking for an entertaining and inspring speaker for your church group, civic organization or corporate function, contact Darrell Huckaby. He is a dynamic speaker--always funny--and can tailor his presentation to fit any occasion. E-mail him today at:

DHuck08@bellsouth.net

or contact him through his website at:

www.darrellhuckaby.net

Your group will be glad you did!

LaVergne, TN USA
06 April 2011
222935LV00001B/2/P